# 5000 HOURS

---
*The ultimate guide to good mental health*
---

# KELVIN SNAITH

Cognitive Behavioural Psychotherapist

and

Founder of Hands up Therapy

### Special thanks to:

Lucy Giles and Iuliana Marin for proof-reading

Saleh Joy for book formatting

Sajjad Ahmad for cover design

A very special thanks to every client (patient) I have worked with.

Without you, this book wouldn't have been written.

# Foreword

## Why this book?

I'm a Cognitive Behavioural Psychotherapist and, at the time of writing this, have been working for 5 years in an NHS primary care talking therapy service in Poole, Dorset.

For the past 5 years, I have worked with, on average, 24 patients per week who are experiencing depression and/or anxiety disorders and utilised a Cognitive Behavioural Therapy approach to assist these patients in better understanding and managing their symptoms. I calculated this to be over 5000 hours of individual face to face therapy completed with patients.

Having completed 5 years of psychotherapy work, an opportunity presented itself for me to take a sabbatical from work. I seized the opportunity as for some time I had been wanting to pursue some other ventures and goals. One of these goals was to write a self-help book summarising all of my learning from therapy work to date. I considered that this book could then offer an immediately accessible self-help treatment solution to people experiencing symptoms of depression and/or anxiety who are waiting for treatment within a talking therapy service (which can often take many months), or to those who have no access to treatment.

This book has been written as simply as possible, removing any fancy psychological language so that you can understand as quickly as possible what you need to do to start achieving great mental health

It is recommended that you take your time to digest/assimilate the information presented within this book, in addition to making daily time for practice of the methods recommended. Practice makes perfect and is the only way to become confident in the methods presented.

The book starts by introducing the basics: emotions and thoughts with methods to better manage these. There is then a selection of the 'hottest' topics from my therapy room over the past 5 years, which are designed to give some guidance/pointers if a particular hot topic is relevant for you at the moment. The hot topics can be skimmed or skipped if you feel one is not so appropriate for you at the moment.

My hope is that this book will become your 'GO TO' and only book necessary to achieve great mental health for life, saving you thousands of hours and pounds spent on therapy, courses, and study.

So let's begin...

# Contents

The Basics ............................................................................. 1

Hot Topics ........................................................................ 16

   Happiness .................................................................. 17

   Not good enough ...................................................... 23

   Confidence ................................................................ 26

   Motivation ................................................................ 31

   I'm right, you're wrong ............................................. 34

   I'm too fat/skinny .................................................... 36

   Love ........................................................................... 40

   Missing you ............................................................... 43

   Loneliness ................................................................. 47

   I'm ugly ..................................................................... 49

   Family ....................................................................... 53

   Suicidal thinking ...................................................... 56

   Managers from hell .................................................. 59

   Self-harm .................................................................. 65

   Health anxiety and death ......................................... 69

   Worst shame and forgiving self ................................ 77

   Evil people and criminals ......................................... 82

   I can't trust anyone ................................................... 86

Let down ...................................................................89

I'm sorry....................................................................95

Parenting ..................................................................98

Jealousy ..................................................................101

Diet and exercise ....................................................111

I'm stupid................................................................115

Sleep........................................................................119

Career......................................................................124

Pain and sickness....................................................128

Dating and relationships..........................................132

Uncertainty.............................................................140

Addictions ..............................................................144

Obsessive-compulsive rituals/behaviour ....................149

Don't know what I want anymore.............................155

Don't know why I'm feeling this way ........................161

Feeling numb..........................................................165

Panic ......................................................................169

Conclusion and well wishes.......................................173

Appendices.................................................................175

## The Basics

If you want to have good mental health, it is really important you get good at dealing with two things:

1. Emotions
2. Thoughts

Let's start with emotions. What are they?

Emotions are strong reactions that we feel in our body and head at times. They can feel like:

- An energy in the body or head;
- Physical symptoms such as an increased heart rate, butterflies in the stomach, restricted breathing or tense muscles;
- Racing thoughts, confusion, or no thoughts (mind going blank).

How you respond to your emotions is really important and can make the difference between you experiencing acute (for a brief moment) emotions or enduring (keeps coming back) emotions.

NOTE: All emotions are acute (short-lived) but can re-trigger (return) again if we don't understand the thinking that is associated with them, which can make them feel like they are lasting a long time. Recurrent emotional states can often be referred to as moods.

Depression would be an example of this.

There is some debate amongst psychologists about how many emotions there are. For this book, I will not be so concerned about this, but more with trying to label the most commonly presenting emotions in my therapy room over the last five years. I refer to these emotions as the 'BIG 5'. These are:

- Anxiety (Fear) (can include panic)
- Sadness
- Anger
- Shame/Guilt
- Excitement

Most patients I have worked with can identify with these 'Big 5' emotions. There are certainly many other feelings that we could talk about, and that's okay. I have found, however, when exploring other feelings and words, they often merge into one or more of these 'Big 5' emotions.

It is widely accepted amongst psychologists that it is very healthy and normal for human beings to experience a wide variety of emotions throughout their lives. Some suggest that the wider the variety of emotions someone experiences, the healthier they are. Furthermore, if we experience very few emotions, it could be a sign of ill-health.

It is also accepted amongst psychologists that taking an 'accepting approach' to emotions when they arise is best. Unfortunately, little guidance is given by society on how best to achieve this.

## Why is it important to take an 'accepting approach' to emotions when they arise?

Imagine that you are sitting in a waiting room and there is a ticking clock on the wall above your head. Now imagine that you start mentally resisting or battling the sound of the ticking clock. What do you think would start to happen inside of you?

Hopefully, you were able to consider that you may start to feel a bit 'agitated' inside and become a bit 'tense' in your muscles. You may also start to struggle to be able to concentrate on anything else but the sound of the ticking clock.

The same can be true when we try to resist or battle with emotions that have come into our body and head.

## What happens when we resist/battle with emotions that have come into our body and head?

Like in the ticking clock example just mentioned, when we resist or battle with our emotions, we can start to feel a bit distressed. We get tense in our muscles and feel 'agitated' inside. Our focus of attention can shift to the emotions, and so we can struggle to concentrate on anything else. When our muscles are tight, it can be more difficult to breathe freely, and so levels of oxygen and other gasses in our body can change. This change in levels of oxygen and other gasses in our body can trigger an alarm in our nervous system. Our bodies are built to survive, and just like on an airplane, when the oxygen levels drop and the oxygen masks fall down, our bodies detect when levels of gasses within our body change/become unhealthy and react accordingly to try to correct the situation. Mostly, our breathing and heart rate increase in order to restore healthier levels of oxygen and other gases in the body. Blood (which carries oxygen) is pushed around the body by the heart and circulatory system more quickly, while growth and repair mechanisms of the body shut down. Digestion, immune, and logical thinking processes are suppressed because these aren't considered a priority if we are trying to survive. This is why it can be very difficult to think logically/rationally when we are feeling quite emotionally distressed or panicky.

When we are feeling tense and experiencing stress reactions in the body, it can be difficult to feel any calm or relaxed feeling. This can then trigger further anxiety/worry that we will never feel good again.

## Why would we resist/battle with emotions that have come into our body and head?

From an early age, society teaches us that some emotions are 'bad' and that we should try to avoid these at all costs. This learning sets us up to resist or battle with any emotions we perceive as 'bad'. Some commonly perceived 'bad' emotions are: anger, sadness, anxiety, and shame/guilt. Some people have even learned that 'excitement' is a bad emotion and should therefore be suppressed and not experienced.

## How to tackle the resistance and stress reaction that can happen when perceived 'bad' emotions enter the body and mind?

The simplest way to tackle the resistance and stress reaction is:

1. Slow deep breathing;

2. Stop battling/resisting emotions by using the 'hands up' method.

**Slow deep breathing:**

I have found from experience that breathing techniques can quite quickly start to be used as just another 'emotional avoidance' strategy. I, therefore, do not teach any specific breathing techniques but simply encourage my patients to try to take some slow deep breaths. I will usually advise: Imagine that you are breathing in through a tube deep down in your belly. Breathe in as much as you can and then slowly exhale all of the air out. Repeat this process. I have found that keeping breathing instructions as simple as possible can prevent breathing from becoming just another emotional avoidance strategy. I always teach breathing in conjunction with the below hands up method for stopping battling/resisting emotions because without that, breathing is quite ineffective.

**Stop battling/resisting emotions by using the 'hands up' method:**

A really simple method to stop battling/resisting emotions is to consider the following analogy of 'surrendering'. Imagine being stood in a bank when a masked robber comes into the bank pointing what looks like a real gun at everyone. He shouts, 'Put your hands up where I can see them!' What would you do?

If you want to live, you would most probably put your hands up in a 'surrender' fashion so that the robber can clearly see them. When the robber sees that you mean no harm to him and that you are not going to fight him, hopefully he will let you live, take what he needs, and get out of there.

Likewise, when you have an emotion that has come into your body and mind, see it that you are not going to battle with it – surrender to it (remember your oxygen levels depend on it!) – because this is going to allow it to pass in the quickest time possible. The emotion will peak and quite quickly burn down to nothing.

When alone, you can practice this exercise by literally putting your hands up in the air (in a surrender pose) whilst taking some slow deep breaths. If you are around people, it may not be appropriate to put your hands up in a surrender pose as this would likely draw unnecessary attention to yourself, and people may start to suspect you have gone mad. If you are around people, you can imagine an image of yourself in this surrender pose whilst you do some slow deep breaths or simply look at your open palms, which could be resting quite discreetly on your thighs to engage the brain in this process, whilst again taking some slow deep breaths.

You can imagine your fingers represent a percentage gage. Each finger represents 10 percent. All fingers open (100%) would therefore mean that you have completely surrendered or stopped fighting/battling with your emotions/feelings. All fingers closed so that you are making two fists (0%) would mean that you are extremely resisting/fighting with your emotions/feelings. The aim is to fully surrender to your emotions/feelings. You can use your fingers to really help engage the brain in this process. This revolutionary 'hands up' approach to emotions was discovered through my work with many hundreds of patients experiencing depression and anxiety disorders over the last decade. It has proven to be very effective. I have produced apps to teach this simple approach, and these are available on the app stores. There is a free app for Android called 'Hands Up Therapy' and a free app for iOS called 'Hands Up Therapy Lite'. There is also an ad-free paid version (costs less than £1) of the app for iOS called 'Hands Up Therapy'. These apps guide you via simple step by step instructions so that you can become confident in utilising what I refer to in this book as the 'hands up and breathe skill' whenever you need it. Please visit the website: www.handsuptherapy.com for more information.

**Let's now move on to Thoughts.**

Being human means experiencing thoughts in our head (mind) on a daily basis (unless we are unconscious!).

## What are thoughts?

Thoughts are the streams of words that run through our mind.

These streams of words usually come in one of two forms:

- Statements
- Questions

Another possibility and something people often ask about is 'images' that can come into our head (without any words). These are absolutely valid and very normal; in fact, psychologists have done a lot of research on thoughts in the form of images and even produced treatments that focus on these images. For this next section, we will focus only on thoughts that involve streams of words. Interestingly, the hands up approach introduced earlier for emotions can also be applied to images when they arise. I have found from experience this is often the most helpful strategy when working with someone that experiences a lot of images and subsequent thoughts and emotions.

Let's consider some examples of thoughts to see how they fit the form of either a Statement or Question.

- I'm useless. (Statement)
- I'm never going to be in a better financial situation. (Statement)
- She is so rude. (Statement)
- What if this happens today? (Question)
- Should I do it? (Question)
- Will it ever happen? (Question)

Hopefully, you can see how easy it is to distinguish if a thought is in the form of a question or statement. If the sentence would require a full stop at the end and appears to be stating something, then it is a statement. If the sentence would require a question mark on the end and appears to be asking something, then it is a question.

We have thousands of thoughts on a daily basis, and so we don't need to be concerned with considering the form of every thought we have. It is mostly important to consider the form of our thoughts when we are experiencing strong emotions. The reason for this is because in order to stop emotions from returning, we need to understand and reconsider the thoughts associated with them.

A really simple method or rule of thumb to use when considering your thoughts:

- Question the accuracy of any statements you are having – i.e., How accurate or truthful is this statement?

- Answer any questions you are having.

Let's consider an example of this:

- 'I'm useless.'

If you are having this thought and believing it, it is likely you will feel quite useless and sad. With our method of 'questioning the accuracy of statements', we would consider if this statement is really true. When considering if it is really true, you may conclude: 'No, it isn't. I am useful at a lot of things. It is only a few things that I am focusing on being not so good at in this moment.' You may also conclude: 'With the right practice and knowledge, I could become useful at those things I'm not so good at.' By considering this reappraisal, it may allow you to have some peace with this thought and stop the same emotion/s returning should this thought enter your mind again.

When it comes to questioning statements, I have found the work of a lady called Byron Katie to be particularly helpful. Byron Katie asks 'four questions' which she calls 'the work' to help people reappraise their thoughts. These 4 questions are:

1. Is it true? (Yes or no. If no, move to question 3.)

2. Can you absolutely know that it's true? (Yes or no.)

3. How do you react, what happens, when you believe that thought?

4. Who would you be without the thought?

I have found that Byron Katie's questions are so simple yet highly effective in helping people reappraise statement thoughts. I have added a couple of extra questions to Byron Katie's 4 questions, and these are shown in the Appendices section on the sheet titled 'Questioning your statements'. Please note that there are no rules when it comes to questioning your statements. Sometimes the first question of Byron Katie's 4 questions is enough for people to reappraise a belief; sometimes asking all 4 questions is necessary. You can use the sheet of questions I use with my patients, Byron Katie's 4 questions, or any combination of questions that you find work for you. Play around with the questions to see which ones are powerful in helping you reappraise your statements.

Please do visit Byron Katie's website which has further information about the 4 questions she uses and many other wonderful videos and resources: www.thework.com

Let's consider another example:

- 'What if that happens?'

If you are having this thought and leaving it unanswered, it is highly likely you will start to worry and feel anxious. This thought could keep cycling around in your mind and rearing its head at any opportunity. With our method of 'answering questions', you would consider what the answer to this question is. You may conclude: 'It wouldn't be great, but I have experienced similar scenarios before and managed to get through it, so I would get through it.' By considering the answer to this question, it may allow you to have some peace with this thought when it arises and stop the same emotion/s returning should this thought enter your mind again. Answering questions can sometimes reveal further questions or statements. These should then be written down and worked using the same method.

NOTE: The reason it is so important to apply the 'hands up and breathe' method before considering your thoughts:

Thoughts are connected to emotions. If you are pushing away your emotions, then you are also pushing away your thoughts because they are bound together. It is, therefore, impossible to identify what thoughts you are having when you are pushing your emotions away, and so you are likely to become quite frustrated trying to figure it out. When you stop pushing your emotions away, you stop pushing away the associated thoughts and so it becomes much easier to identify and reappraise the thoughts you are having. Furthermore, it's not possible to understand the cause of an emotion (fire) when the fire is burning fiercely. This is explained more in the later hot topic titled 'Don't know why I'm feeling this way'. Please be sure to read this.

You now have the tools you need to achieve good mental health for life. If you are willing to put in some practice, you will start to notice these methods becoming second-nature, i.e., you won't even have to think about them but just do them automatically whenever you experience strong emotions.

A little poem by Mewlana Jalaluddin Rumi to finish:

*This being human is a guest house.*

*Every morning a new arrival.*

*A joy, a depression, a meanness, some momentary awareness comes as an unexpected visitor.*

*Welcome and entertain them all!*

*Even if they're a crowd of sorrows, who violently sweep your house empty of its furniture, still, treat each guest honourably.*

*He may be clearing you out for some new delight.*

*The dark thought, the shame, the malice, meet them at the door laughing, and invite them in.*

*Be grateful for whoever comes, because each has been sent as a guide from beyond.*

(Taken from 'The Essential Rumi, Translations by Coleman Barks with John Moyne', 1995)

NOTE ABOUT MENTAL HEALTH DISORDERS:

This book purposefully does not directly address individual mental health disorders such as depression, post-traumatic stress disorder (PTSD), generalised anxiety disorder, social anxiety disorder, specific phobias, panic disorder, etc. The reason for this is quite simple: I do not believe it is necessary!

I've come to see that all non-organic mental health disorders involve the 'BIG 5' emotions and 2 types of thoughts (statements and questions) and, more specifically, the unhealthy management of these. If we start to manage our emotions and thoughts in a healthier way, we can start to recover from all non-organic mental health disorders.

I have included a formulation or model for the treatment of all non-organic mental illness in the Appendices section.

# Hot Topics

The following chapters offer a selection of the most common topics that have arisen when working with people over the past five years, at various points throughout therapy. I have offered some pointers and guidance on each of these topics. Feel free to skim or skip any topics that you don't feel are so relevant for you at the moment. I have found that for anyone living a full life, every one of these topics will be relevant at some point.

# Happiness

*'Happiness is your nature. It is not wrong to desire it. What is wrong is seeking it outside when it is inside.'*
~ **Ramana Maharshi**

Perhaps the biggest hot topic of all to present in the therapy room is that of happiness. Pretty much every one of my patients comes with the goal of wanting 'happiness'.

**What is this thing then that we all want?**

Society, and in particular media/advertising, teaches us that happiness comes from material things. When we get that car, designer handbag, or dream holiday/lifestyle, that's when we will feel happy. As a result, we learn that happiness is something that comes with material things. Furthermore, happiness is something that can only be secured if certain things remain.

I would suggest that most people have never actually considered what happiness really is. I will often talk about happiness with my patients and hone in on specific examples from their lives about things that 'make them happy' or have made them happy in the past. I will then ask how they felt inside their body in those specific examples of happiness. People often respond with 'I felt good.' When I inquire more about this 'feeling good' and ask for other words that could possibly describe this, people often will use words such as 'calm' or 'peaceful' or 'relaxed'. People may also advise that they are 'carefree' or 'not worrying' in those happiness examples.

Interestingly then, it seems the 'feeling' of happiness can be described with other words. I would suggest that these other words also describe our very essence or nature, which can be felt when 'emotions' aren't present. Happiness then is another name for our very nature or essence. This is what a lot of spiritual teachers and gurus talk about. (Please also see the hot topic about Love.)

So, if our goal is to get happiness and happiness is the feeling of our essence when emotions have diffused, the simple way to get this is to apply the 'hands up and breathe' skill whenever we are experiencing emotions. We then start to see that it's possible to achieve 'happiness' or 'feeling good' whenever we stop the fight with our emotions. Furthermore, we don't need anything or anyone to give us that. For most, this will be a totally new way of thinking about things. It may also be quite difficult to hear having had a lifetime of conditioning suggesting otherwise.

I advise my patients that there is absolutely nothing we can do about the happiness 'learning' we have already gained, i.e., the learning of what makes us happy. That learning is deeply conditioned into us, and so we cannot stop that. I also advise that the things that 'make us happy' are great gifts from God or the universe, and it's never wrong to want these things in our life. However, there are likely to be times in our life when, for whatever reason, it is not possible to get or do the thing/s that 'make us happy'. This is often the time when people can start to experience mental health problems and present to a counsellor or therapist.

I encourage people to consider their 'learning' of what makes them happy as a kind of 'definition of happiness' and then review how their life is looking against this definition of happiness.

FAILING TO YOUR DEFINITION OF HAPPINESS:

Something I often talk about with patients is 'failing to your definition of happiness' and how it is okay to do this. There may be a good reason why it isn't possible for us to do something that makes us happy, for example, playing a round of golf if we have a broken ankle or going clothes shopping if we have no money. If playing a round of golf a few times a week is in our definition, then we may have to 'fail to our definition' of happiness so long as we have a broken ankle.

Equally, if going clothes shopping once a week is in our definition of happiness, then we may have to 'fail to our definition' so long as we have no money to do this. We don't need to change our definition or pretend that we can be happy without those things as that is not authentic and only likely to contribute to more 'unpeace' and confusion. When we 'accept' that we aren't living up to our definition of happiness currently and hands up and breathe to any emotions present, we can start to feel peace (feeling good) again. We can then learn that it is possible to have 'feeling good' even if we are failing to our definition of happiness. We can also then start to consider that our 'definition' isn't so important, just things that can help to facilitate the feeling of our true essence. We can use these as 'gifts' when they are available but not form an over-reliance on them. We may even find that some things fall away having learnt that they are not 'required' for our 'feeling good'.

## NOTE ABOUT SPIRITUAL SEEKERS AND HAPPINESS:

It is not uncommon for people who have read many self-help type books to develop a new learning in relation to the 'wanting of material things'. This new learning suggests that the 'wanting of material things' is 'wrong'. These people can then pretend they don't want 'material things' anymore in an attempt to show that they are more 'psychologically and/or spiritually evolved'. Similarly, some people can pretend they don't feel 'negative emotions' anymore as they are so 'psychologically/spiritually' advanced. These people are likely to feel even more unhappy than someone relying on material things to facilitate their happiness because until they have learned another way to 'feel good', they will have no way of 'feeling good'. Furthermore, they may be 'avoiding their emotions' more, which only serves to prevent the emotions from being processed and so they will keep returning. Some of these people may report a kind of 'addiction' to self-help type books and attending talks with gurus in order to help them 'feel good' as they may not have any other options to help them 'feel good'. If this is the case, it can be treated just like any other addiction (please read the hot topic about addictions).

I CAN'T BE HAPPY UNTIL...

What naturally comes with our 'definition of happiness' (the things we have learned make us happy) is the thinking (belief) 'I can't be happy until...' These thoughts are easily reappraised after applying the 'hands up and breathe' skill and reconnecting to some 'good feeling'. The good feeling shows us that we don't need anything or anyone to feel good.

## NOTE ABOUT 'MANIFESTING YOUR DREAMS TO ACHIEVE HAPPINESS' SELF-HELP MOVEMENT:

An important difference between the underlying message of this book ('hands up and breathe' skill) and the 'manifesting your dreams' self-help movement is that the 'manifesting your dreams' self-help movement can feed the belief that happiness comes from material things and is therefore outside of yourself, whereas the 'hands up and breathe' skill shows us that happiness is our essence and available right now. I absolutely encourage my patients to work towards their dreams and goals when they can but always hold them lightly in the knowing that we can never have more 'feeling good' than we can have in this moment.

# Not good enough

### 'Is the feeling of peace good enough?'
### ~ K.Snaith

A common theme to present in the therapy room is that of people feeling that they are 'not good enough'. This is very common in patients who have experienced abuse at the hands of others over a long period of time but can also present in people with a more healthy self-esteem at certain times of life.

Relationships, in particular, can trigger thoughts of being 'not good enough', especially if there is a breakup and harsh words have been exchanged.

Old-school parenting styles, which involve no praise or celebration of success, can also contribute to children feeling they are 'not good enough', which can then be carried into adult life.

If this thinking is coming up for you, I invite you to take the following steps:

1. Identify where you feel the feeling of 'not good enough' in the body. See if it is located in a particular

place or it is spread throughout the whole body. Does it have a colour? A temperature? What does it feel like? Try to really connect to the energy of the feeling.

2. Once you have identified the feeling of 'not good enough' in the body, put your hands up to it and breathe. It is important you get to 100 per cent hands up (full surrender) when doing the 'hands up and breathe' skill. Anything less than 100 per cent means you are still resisting/battling your emotions. Take your time and keep going until you fully surrender to the feeling in your body. Remember to take some slow deep breaths whilst doing this.

Applying these 2 steps will allow the 'energy' of 'not good enough' to diffuse. You can then notice what's left in the body. Can you feel the peace again? The 'good' feeling again? I invite you once you have connected to this good feeling again to ask the question, 'Is this good enough?' In my experience, it is very hard for someone to answer 'no' to this question. When we are feeling peace, the brain works better, and we can start to be more rational about things. We can start to consider that 'I'm not good enough' is not a true statement because we are made of 'good' feeling, and this is available always when we are not battling with our emotions. We may also be able to then consider more specifically which aspect of us we think is not good enough. We can then consider that most things we do in life can be improved with the right knowledge, patience, and practice. This subject may also link to the following hot topics:

Confidence

I'm stupid

I'm ugly

I'm too fat/thin.

Please read these also if you are bothered by thoughts of not being good enough.

# Confidence

> 'A great figure or physique is nice, but it's self-confidence that makes someone really sexy.'
> ~ Vivica Fox

As the quote highlights, 'Confidence is sexy!' We all want it, yet most of us have no idea how to get it because we have never examined what it actually is, and so it remains a 'mysterious' force that only a blessed few can achieve. We live in hope that one day we too will be blessed by the mysterious confidence force. Some people create stories about what they think is needed to have confidence, for example, 'If only I can get that, then I will be confident.' Others believe that only God can bless them with the gift of confidence.

What's clear from my work is that so long as confidence remains a 'mysterious force' in our minds, it will continue to be unachievable.

If I received a pound every time I heard the expression 'I don't have any confidence', I'd be quite a rich man now. When I hear this expression, my first question back to the person saying it is, 'In anything?' The look I get is usually quite a puzzled one. What I'm asking the person to consider is if their statement is true in every aspect of their life. Often, people will still reply with, 'Yes, that's right.' I will then ask, 'Are you confident in boiling the kettle?' or 'Are you confident in doing up your shirt on a morning?' or 'Are you confident in making a cup of tea?' Usually, then people will laugh and say, 'Yes, of course.' So then we have clarified, their very broad statement simply isn't true. They are confident in some things but not confident in others. We can then go about clarifying further what exactly they feel they are not confident in and then writing those more specific statements down.

At this point, I usually share a little story to help us further consider what confidence is.

This story is about a trainee mechanic called Adam:

There once was a trainee mechanic called Adam. His manager had asked him to change the head gasket on an engine. Adam had never done this before and didn't even know where or what the head gasket of the engine was. Would you expect Adam to feel confident in changing the head gasket at this point?

Adam expressed to his manager that he didn't know how to do this job, and so the manager gave him a detailed instruction manual, which details step by step exactly how to change the head gasket in an engine. Adam perused the manual from cover to cover and even read it twice to ensure that he had understood it. Would you expect Adam to feel confident in changing the head gasket at this point?

Adam was feeling more confident to attempt the task now that he had read the instruction manual, and so he went ahead with the task utilising the knowledge he had gained from reading the instruction manual. Surely enough, with some slow and steady work, Adam was able to successfully complete the task. Would you expect Adam to feel confident in changing the head gasket at this point?

Hopefully, you were able to consider that having done the job successfully, Adam's confidence will have been boosted. However, unfortunately for Adam, his nagging mind creeps in soon after completing the job and starts saying, 'You were just lucky that time, you couldn't do it again!' As a result of these doubting thoughts, Adam's confidence is now waning.

Adam attempts to do the job again on another car to see if he can put his nagging mind to rest. He is successful in doing the job again. What do you think Adam's confidence will be like now?

Unfortunately for Adam, his nagging mind then creeps in again, saying that 'It still may just be luck as you have only done it 2 times.' As a result, Adam's confidence is knocked again, and so he decides to give it a try on a third car.

On successfully completing the third car, Adam was feeling really confident that he now could change the head gasket in an engine.

The moral of the story:

Until Adam has the right knowledge to do the job (read instruction manual) and given himself enough evidence through practice (as a rule of thumb, at least 3 times of successfully doing something in a recent time period), he is unable to feel fully confident.

The good news:

Confidence does not have to be a 'mysterious' force that is only achievable to a blessed few. Confidence is actually quite easy to achieve by all once you understand its requirements.

I have come up with a simple equation to apply whenever you are wanting more confidence in something.

CONFIDENCE EQUATION:

Confidence = Knowledge + recent Practice

Whenever you feel you are lacking confidence and want some more confidence, the first thing to do is:

1. BE SPECIFIC

Be specific about exactly what it is you are not feeling confident in.

Then,

2. Go to the Confidence Equation and check if you are meeting the requirements for confidence; i.e., do you have the knowledge required to do what you want to do and also recent practice doing that thing?

If you are missing knowledge or recent practice, then you will need to go about achieving these components of the equation. Confidence will then be yours.

There is a slight crossover when talking about Confidence with a hot topic later in the book called 'Too fat/Too thin'. Please also see this chapter for some more specific pointers on 'body confidence'.

# Motivation

*'Motivation is simply a good reason for doing something.'*
*~ K.Snaith*

For most, motivation is something that cannot be understood and is something that just happens at times and doesn't at other times. Similar to confidence, motivation has an air of 'mysterious force'. Most people live in hope that they will be 'motivated' when they need to be and complain when they aren't motivated.

Similar to confidence, motivation is actually achievable by all when we know how.

Here is where I tell the story of Jack:

Jack is a single young man that is on the lookout for a single young lady. Jack would like to have a serious relationship and is prepared to do what it takes to achieve this.

Like any young man, Jack is quite concerned about his appearance and so decides that if he is to find an attractive girlfriend, he needs to be in the best shape he can be in. Jack's reason to find a girlfriend is a great reason for him to get into the gym and workout. Jack finds that for the next few months, he is very motivated and gets to the gym regularly.

One day when Jack was leaving the gym, he met a lady who was waiting in the reception area. They got chatting and agreed to go on a date sometime. A few months later and Jack found himself in a very happy relationship with this lady, and things were going great.

What wasn't going so great was that Jack suddenly found himself without any motivation to go to the gym. Jack couldn't understand why he had lost all of his motivation for the gym as he had been so disciplined in getting there most days of the week for the last few months.

What do you think has happened to Jack's motivation?

Hopefully, you were able to consider that Jack's good reason for going to the gym, i.e., to get in good shape so he can find an attractive girlfriend, is no longer motivating him because he has now found a girlfriend. It's therefore totally normal and understandable that Jack currently doesn't feel any motivation for the gym. Until Jack can find a new good reason for him to continue going to the gym, he will not have any motivation.

I have created a very simple equation that you can use whenever you find yourself lacking in motivation.

MOTIVATION EQUATION:

MOTIVATION = A GOOD REASON FOR DOING SOMETHING

Below are the simple steps in applying this equation.

1. Be Specific

Like confidence, it is very important to first specifically identify where you are lacking motivation. Write it down.

2. Consider the equation and if you are currently meeting it, i.e., Do you have a good reason for doing something? Consider this carefully. Often, we can think we have a good reason for doing something, but with some further questioning, it doesn't hold up. Ultimately, the proof of whether your reason is good enough or not will be in the results, i.e., does it get you doing something?

IMPORTANT NOTE: Addictions may serve to block motivation, and so it is worth reviewing the hot topic titled 'Addictions'.

# I'm right, you're wrong

**'Would you rather be right or free?'**
**~ Byron Katie.**

The story of 'I'm right, you're wrong' goes like this:

[SHOUTING] 'I'm right, you're wrong!' (Slams door as leaves room)

We all know this scenario, right?

I've come to see that living from this position is a very limited way of living. Why do I say this? Because when we live from this position, there is no way of growing (for both involved), even if there is better, more accurate knowledge to be gained. It distances us from other people, potentially even ruining some friendships/relationships for good.

I'd like for you to consider the following if you are one of those that often thinks 'I'm right, they're wrong':

If you are so confident you are right, what would it cost you to hear someone's reasons out? Surely they are just going to expose their inaccurate knowledge/information when talking, which will only serve to confirm what you already knew: that you are right! It will also allow you to better understand the knowledge that they have so that you can then fill in the blanks needed for them to be able to understand your position. This means that someone is more likely to come around to your way of thinking by really hearing them out. Furthermore, what if your knowledge was out-of-date and there was some better, more accurate knowledge to be gained? Wouldn't you want to hear about this? Learning new information may help you to live a better life and really benefit you.

# I'm too fat/skinny

'The size of your body has nothing to do with peace.'
~ K. Snaith

From an early age, we learn from the media what is considered to be the perfect looking male and female physique.

It's important to realise if you are having thoughts such as 'I'm too thin' or 'I'm too fat' that it is simply your mind making a comparison to what you have been led to believe is the perfect looking male/female physique. On a surface level, the thought may appear quite true when compared to the image of 'perfect' you have learned. However, when you consider that the image of 'perfect' you are comparing to is purely 'made up' by the media, it becomes harder to hold up as fact.

The media slowly seems to be displaying a wider variety of female model body types, which is helping to challenge the conditioned belief about what is the 'perfect' female body. It seems that, sadly, such variety is still not emerging for male model physiques. Interestingly, eating disorders, anorexia nervosa, and body dysmorphic disorder are more prevalent than ever in men and appear to be on the rise.

I use a very simple exercise to challenge the thinking related to being 'too thin' or 'too fat'.

Let's start with the thinking 'I'm too fat':

Take a moment to consider 5 people who are quite a lot fatter than you. These have to be real people that you know or have seen in the media recently. An instant response when inviting people to do this exercise is 'I can't do it' or 'I don't want to do that'. When I ask why, people will often say they feel bad about doing this. I usually advise that we are in no way putting these people down or thinking bad of them in any way; we are simply highlighting their body fat levels as being higher than our own.

Once you have identified 5 people, I would like for you to line them all up in your mind and then put yourself next to them.

I'd like for you to then consider, how do you compare to these 5 people? Could it be just as true, if not more true now, that compared to these people you are 'thin'?

This simple exercise can be a very powerful restructurer of the thought 'I'm too fat' because often what holds up this thought or belief is images of people 'thinner' than you being displayed in your mind.

Once we have gained some perspective that there are always people fatter and thinner than us, we can see that we have a choice as to what thought we believe. A healthier thought may be, 'I could be fatter, and I could be thinner; right now, I'm the size I am supposed to be.'

The same exercise can be done if you are having the thought 'I'm too thin'.

Take a moment to consider 5 real people that you know or have seen in the media recently who are thinner than you. Again, line them up in your mind and then put yourself next to them. Consider, how do you compare to these? Could it be just as true, if not more true now, that compared to these people you are quite 'fat'? Again consider, there are always people fatter and thinner than us, and so it could be healthier to think that 'I could be fatter, and I could be thinner; right now, I'm the size that I am supposed to be.'

Having done these simple exercises, we can start to consider that the 'perfect' male or female body isn't a fact; it is simply a conditioned idea that has been created by the media. We can still be attractive even if we fall short of the conditioned beauty standard. It's important to note also that we do have the power to change our body through exercise/working out and eating more or less food. This can be experimented with, but I would suggest that you approach your experimenting by always remembering that the 'media ideal' is fictional and not fact. This will help you to keep some balance and perspective in your experimenting.

# Love

> 'If you wish to find love, don't look for the object of love but rather for the source of love. There you will find the beloved.'
>
> ~ Mooji

What is love?

Dictionary says:

love ləv/

*Noun*

1. An intense feeling of deep affection.

I would suggest that Love is no more than our very essence, our true self, when the mind is clear and quiet.

I would suggest that most people experience glimpses of love when growing up in moments of 'no mind' which can be experienced during certain activities or situations. These activities or situations are great blessings. Love can often first be experienced with another human being.

Things get a bit confusing when we wrongly attribute the source of love to be coming from another person or thing, rather than recognise it to be coming from our own essence or self.

Love is synonymous to peace, joy, or happiness. All these words are one and the same, and all relate to our very essence or self.

Love is often confused with 'Lust'. Lust is what we feel when we are sexually excited and wanting someone sexually.

Love is also often associated with 'romance', what appears to be two people doing nice things together in order to get to know each other better.

Love often comes with its own set of beliefs, which have usually come from society and family. Here are a few common beliefs associated with love:

- If you love someone, you are meant to be together.//
- If you love someone, you should do anything for them (can even include dying for someone if necessary).
- If you love someone, you should always agree with each other and think in the same way.

- If you love someone, you should always want to do the same things at the same time.
- If you love someone, you should always want to have sex.

If love is coming up as an important topic for you, I'd recommend some 'hands up and breathe' time with any emotions being experienced about the topic. Then consider and write down what you have learned about love so far and your beliefs about love. Take your time to question your statements and answer any questions.

As your beliefs about love are questioned, they slowly drop away. What is left when the mind drops away? As Mooji so nicely put it, 'the source of love', there you will find the beloved.

Please also read the hot topic on 'Dating and relationships' as this very much links to this hot topic.

# Missing you

> 'If you look too closely at the form, you miss the essence.'
> ~ Rumi

A very common thought arising in patients I have worked with is 'I miss him/her.' Most people have experienced this thought at some point in their lives, particularly after a breakup in a relationship or when a loved one passes away.

Society actually teaches us from an early age that 'missing' someone is a very romantic and a nice thing to do. Love songs, movies, music, and books will often talk about 'missing' someone. For this reason, we rarely question the thought/belief of 'missing' someone because we consider it to be reasonable to continue believing this thought.

The first thing I always invite people to consider with this subject is the meaning of the word 'miss'. The word miss is often used in the English language to describe 'not seeing' something, for example, 'I missed the turning' or 'I missed my keys on the way out.' In these examples, we have failed to see the turning or keys, i.e., we have not seen something. If we then consider how we use the word 'miss' in some of our thoughts, it doesn't make so much sense.

'I miss him.' So what we are saying here is, I have 'failed to see' him. How accurate is this when you are thinking of an ex-partner, for example, aren't you seeing lots of images in your head of the partner before the thought 'I miss him' arose? So actually, you were seeing lots of him (images of him) in that moment before the thought arrived, which stated 'I miss him.'

In this sense, 'I miss him/her' is never a true thought. It can't be, because you always see images of the person before the thought arises. What may be more true to say is that you are 'remembering/recalling' lots of images of that person right now and maybe more so, thinking about how you would like to have some of those experiences again. Although a subtle reframe, I would suggest this reframe provides much less of an emotional reaction and allows you to feel more peace. It also gives the opportunity to question the statement, 'I would like to have that again.' Often, this thought is not true when questioned. If you are revising for an important exam, is it really true at that moment that you want to be doing something with your ex-partner? Questioning the thought in this way may help to ward it off. There may be some moments when even after questioning the thought, it feels very true. For example, perhaps you are alone one evening and watching tv when the thought arises that you are 'missing' snuggling with your partner like the two of you used to do. Reframing the 'missing' thought may help somewhat, but you may find it hard to ward off the thought of 'wanting to have that experience right now' as you aren't particularly doing much else other than watching tv. What may be important to consider in a moment like this is, 'do you have faith in the universe or God's plans? Do you want to run the universe? Maybe we aren't meant to have that experience right now because we need to be freed up to have another experience? Can you trust in God's or the universal plans? This links somewhat to the hot topic of 'I'm right, you're wrong.'

There is an even deeper reflection and questioning that can occur with the thought 'I miss him/her.'

This relates to the bigger question of 'who' we actually are and also 'who' other people are. When we talk about 'him' or 'her', who are we actually referring to? Are we referring to the flesh and bones, the mind, or the essence of that someone?

What is it about their flesh and bones, mind, or essence that we miss so much?

I put it to you that it is always about how you feel inside when you are around that person. So it's actually more true to say that what you are really missing is the feeling you had inside when you were around that person.

What was the feeling you had inside when you were around that person?

Was it love, happiness, peace, joy, or calm?

Are these not words for our essence?

It's possible then, when we consider it, that these people we are 'missing' are actually people that gave us the opportunity to feel our true essence. This is a very beautiful thing, and those people are a great blessing. However, only a confused mind could suggest these people are needed for this feeling. This links to the hot topic of 'Love', and so you may also want to read that again after this one.

When we see that nobody is giving us anything, we are only ever feeling our true essence. It's possible to consider that we, therefore, can't ever be missing that.

When we work on silencing the mind by questioning our statements and answering our questions, we are left with essence – pure love – which has nothing to do with anyone or anything else.

# Loneliness

> 'The cure for loneliness? Feel.'
> ~ K.Snaith

Loneliness has nothing to do with people and everything to do with your willingness to feel.

People live in cities or a busy household and may be surrounded constantly by people yet feel great loneliness. In contrast, someone may live alone in a house on a small island and see hardly any people all day or night yet feel at perfect peace.

Loneliness is, therefore, the specific story of 'lacking' someone in your life. The story that you are 'incomplete' and 'needing' someone else to help you to feel better. It is an incredibly powerful feeling and has been linked with ill health and even increased risk of suicide. Where hope has started to decline, suicidal thoughts can start to arise.

See the hot topic on suicidal thinking for further pointers on this.

Questioning the 'lacking' thought to see where you have started to play the role of God/universe in deciding what's best for your life can help dismantle the thought and allow it to fall away. Key question: Am I sure I want to take on the role of God or the universe in deciding how my life should be right now?

I have found from experience that an even quicker way of working the feeling of loneliness is to 'hands up' to the feeling directly when it arises. See how lonely you can feel. Can you totally surrender and allow the loneliness? Can you let the loneliness peak (reach its maximum burning point) and watch as it starts to fall? Doing this takes you right back to what's always underneath feelings, our essence – the peace and love, which can then act as the greatest restructurer of the thought that you are 'lacking' someone or something. In many cases, I have found that the need to question thoughts becomes redundant when we properly apply the 'hands up and breathe' skill. The thoughts are effortlessly restructured by the mind when the feeling of essence – love/peace – is reconnected to.

This subject can also very much link to the hot topic titled 'Missing someone'.

# I'm ugly

'Could you be uglier?'
~ K.Snaith

Most of us, at some point in our life, will experience the thought 'I'm ugly.' For some, this thought may occur on a weekly, daily, or even more frequent basis.

This hot topic can also link to the hot topic 'I'm too fat/thin'. As highlighted in that hot topic, when it comes to beauty, we are all brainwashed. From an early age, society, and in particular the media (tv/magazines, etc.), teaches us what is considered 'beautiful' and what is considered 'ugly'. Models in the media dictate to us on a daily basis what is considered 'beautiful' and so we can't help but compare ourselves to these models. If we consider that we compare okay to the models we see in the media, i.e., look similar to them, we may consider that we must also be beautiful. If we consider that we don't compare well to the models, i.e., look very different to them, we may consider that we must be ugly.

What's important to consider then is that the definition of 'beautiful' and 'ugly' has been created by society, and in particular by the media; therefore, it isn't a fact. Definitions of 'beautiful' and 'ugly' can change as models change, and this is very evident in different parts of the world. A simple example I give for this would be skin colour in India and in England. In India, if someone has dark brown skin, it is considered that this person must be a lower-class person, i.e., they may be someone with a poorly paid job that works outdoors on the street in the hot sun (which is why their skin has turned dark brown), and maybe they cannot afford a place to live even. If someone has paler brown skin, the person is considered higher class because it is assumed they don't work in the hot sun all day in a poorly paid job and can afford good housing. As a result of this thinking, paler brown skin is considered much more beautiful and attractive to most Indian people. This thinking is so common that skin bleaching products and even supplements are rife throughout India.

In direct contrast to this, tanned (brown) skin in England is considered very beautiful and attractive. Perhaps the reason is the opposite to that in India; i.e., if people have brown skin in England, it may be assumed to mean that those people are wealthy enough to take lots of nice holidays abroad in warmer climates, whereas if someone has very pale white skin, they may not have the money to be able to go away to warmer places. As a result, a massive 'brown skin' industry can be found in England, where people can attend 24-hour tanning salons or buy supplements and beauty products to get browner skin.

Another example I give is that of a small tribe in South America which considers big noses to be a sign of intelligence. In this one tribe, if you have a big nose, you are considered to be very beautiful and attractive because you are highly intelligent. Contrastly, in England, a big nose may be considered quite ugly because many models in the media may have very small noses giving the impression that small noses are beautiful. As a result, millions of pounds are spent each year by British citizens on 'nose jobs' to make their noses appear smaller.

These examples highlight nicely the fragility of the beautiful/ugly standards and how, depending on where you find yourself in the world, you may be considered beautiful or ugly.

Another simple exercise I do to challenge the 'I'm ugly' thinking is:

Take a moment to consider 5 people you know or have seen in the media recently that you think are uglier than you.

Once you have considered 5 people, line them up in your mind's eye and put yourself next to these people. Now consider, could it be just as true, if not more true, compared to these people that you are beautiful?

People often report feeling quite uncomfortable when doing this exercise because they consider it isn't nice or unkind in some way to do this exercise. My response to this is that we aren't thinking badly about these people; we are simply doing an exercise that involves comparing appearances to a conditioned or created beauty standard.

I also point out that we have no problem comparing ourselves to people we consider to be more beautiful than us, yet we feel uncomfortable comparing ourselves to people we consider to be more ugly than us. Why is this?

A deeper questioning could also occur in relation to who the 'I' is in 'I'm ugly'. Are we 'flesh and bones' or something deeper? When we see that what we are is peace/love/relaxed feeling, we see that this can never be considered ugly, and so the thought just doesn't hold up.

# Family

> 'Families are made up of people, and unfortunately, people don't always manage their thoughts and emotions in a healthy way.'
> ~ K.Snaith

One of the most common hot topics to arise with my patients is that of family. Perhaps the reason for this is that nearly all of us have family, even if it is acquired family through a relationship we are in.

The first point I always like to make about family is that families are made up of people, and people are not always awake to their thoughts and emotions and/or managing their thoughts and emotions in a healthy way. This means that potentially family members could be a little bit 'crazy' or have very poor mental health/emotional coping skills, which can make them really difficult to get on with. Until someone has learned the 'hands up and breathe' skill, along with the 'questioning/answering your thoughts' skill, it is highly unlikely they will have optimal mental health.

Most of us have learned from a very early age that 'family should stick together, no matter what' and that 'blood is thicker than water'. This is by far the most common childhood instilled belief about family I have observed from working with patients over the last 5 years. This belief seems to get passed from generation to generation without any questioning.

What these family beliefs indirectly imply is that 'I should always get on with family, no matter what', furthermore, 'whatever they do, I should just put up with it /accept it'. This is a very potent recipe for distress because, in reality, we don't get along with all people, and neither do we want to put up with all things.

I would suggest that it is highly likely you will not get on with all your family members; furthermore, it would really be quite extraordinary if you did. Considering this reappraisal thought, along with the fact that family members are just 'people', can immediately start to offer some relief from any 'family distress' that you may be experiencing.

I like to point out to my patients when talking about family that even the word 'family' is a little unquestioned. What does family even mean? Blood-related? Closely genetically connected? Well, aren't we all blood or genetically related if you look far enough back? We all belong to the human being species, and so in that sense, we are all biologically connected. When we see this, we realise the silliness of suggesting that we should be able to get on with and put up with a few people no matter how they are or what they do because they are genetically related to us.

Most people are able to consider quite instantly that we cannot get on with all people. The blocking point when it comes to their 'family' is the deeply held belief/s that oppose the reality of not getting on with all people.

# Suicidal thinking

> 'Of course you would start to consider being better off dead if that is the feeling you have to live with on a regular basis.'
> ~K.Snaith

When we experience an emotion or unpleasant feeling repeatedly for some time, it's totally normal and even healthy for us to start to consider that we don't want to feel that way anymore. If we don't have the skills to change the feeling, we may then start to lose hope that things will ever be any different and/or that we will ever feel any different. When this starts to happen, it's quite understandable we may start to consider 'if this is how I'm going to feel forever, maybe I'd be better off dead.'

Seeing that your suicidal thinking is simply connected to losing hope that you will ever feel any different can help you to start to feel better because you are understanding why it is happening. Learning the 'hands up and breathe' skill when you are experiencing strong emotions and how to question/answer your thoughts empowers you with the skills you need to change how you feel. In this sense, these skills offer the best preventative treatment and treatment for suicidal thinking.

Whilst considering suicidal thinking, it may also be worth considering why some people act on suicidal thoughts to end their life. I would suggest that when it comes to taking action, it's not so much to do with loss of hope but more about 'reasons for living'.

I have worked with many people, particularly at the start of therapy, who report no hope at all that things could change or that they will feel any different, yet they had not and were not taking any action to end their life. The reason for this is that they reported when questioned 'good enough' reason/s to stay alive. Despite reporting feeling more or less 'dead' inside, they continued to carry on because of their good enough reason/s to live. The cases I encountered where people had taken action to end their life reported no hope that things or feelings could change and also no 'good enough' reason/s to stay alive.

It can be quite scary to start to consider what is my reason to stay alive when already feeling very emotional, but I have found from experience that considering our reason/s to stay alive can be quite life-changing. It can help to get our life back on track, in line with our heart and values.

If you are experiencing suicidal thinking and, furthermore, you are unable to identify any reason/s for living, please take your time to do lots of hands up and breathing skill, ensuring that you get to 100 per cent hands up (surrender). Feeling some calm/peace offers the best evidence and restructuring of 'hopeless' thinking. It is also more possible to consider your reason/s for living and what changes, if any, need to be made to your life when feeling some calm/relaxed feeling. If you find yourself still unable to identify any reason/s for living, you may need to revisit this subject a few more times over the coming days. This work can take time. Don't rush it. I regularly report to my patients that for some thoughts, I have taken many days, even weeks, to reflect before reaching an answer/statement that feels balanced, true, and peaceful. If you have reflected over several days and still have not reached any answers/statements that feel balanced, true, and peaceful, you can always seek additional support from an experienced counsellor/therapist. There is never any shame in this. I often advise there is great benefit in holding out with this work before seeking additional support, in order to gain confidence in your own ability to work your thoughts/emotions, but please do not hesitate to seek support from a therapist or counsellor (maybe even several) before taking an irreversible action such as that of ending your life.

# Managers from hell

*'If in the darkness of ignorance, you don't recognize a person's true nature, look to see whom he/she has chosen for his/her leader.'*

*~ Rumi*

Most working adults who are employed will likely experience the dreaded 'manager from hell' at some point in their career. Some may already have encountered the manager from hell and still be recovering from the experience.

Managers from hell are managers that appear to be quite evil people. They appear to want to make your life a misery and won't stop until they have achieved this.

I have worked with many hundreds of patients who are suffering at the hands of managers from hell and/or still trying to heal and recover from previous managers from hell.

Managers from hell appear to be evil people, and this hot topic therefore very much links to the hot topic of 'Evil people and criminals', which can also be read. I'm making it a seperate hot topic in addition to 'Evil people and criminals' because of how commonly this subject presents in my therapy room.

The first thing I usually spend some time considering with patients experiencing managers from hell is whether their managers really are evil people. The reason I start to immediately consider this with patients is that I have found from experience that to believe a manager, or anyone, is an evil person is actually quite unhelpful.

How does it make you feel when you really believe your manager is an evil person?

Do you notice how your defences immediately come up? Maybe you feel quite scared inside? Maybe you feel quite confused, anxious, angry, stressed, tense? Maybe you want to run away but can't, so you feel trapped? I invite you to consider how does your mind function when you are experiencing any or all of these feelings? Can you work as effectively? Can you reason and discuss things as effectively? Can you deal with your problems as effectively?

Hopefully, you are able to consider that when we are experiencing any of these heightened emotions or feelings, it is hard for us to function as effectively. We, therefore, aren't likely to be doing our job as well or problem-solve so effectively, which is only going to annoy our manager even more. It's a vicious cycle.

As with all the hop topics in this book, the first thing I encourage you to do is take your time in doing some hands up and breathing to the emotions and feelings you are experiencing. Let the feelings peak/max out and then start to fall. Let some peace start to return into your body as you continue to breathe deeply. Connecting to some peace is going to allow your mind to work more effectively.

Some key questions I always ask in relation to managers from hell are, 'How well do you think your manager is managing his/her emotions and mental health? Do you think your manager has good mental health? Do you think your manager knows about the 'hands up and breathe' method and is applying it? Do you think your manager is questioning his/her statements and answering questions?'

In my experience, managers from hell don't have good mental health. They don't appear to be managing their emotions in a healthy way, most probably because they have not yet gained the knowledge of how to manage their emotions in a healthy way. It's important to consider that interviewers may not have asked your manager about his/her 'emotional coping skills' and mental health when interviewed. This may not have been seen as an 'essential criteria' on the job specification.

It's important to consider that most people don't have healthy emotional management skills because we don't learn these in school or from society. For most of us, the first time we will learn healthy emotional management strategies is when we experience mental health problems!

Hopefully, you are now starting to consider an alternative hypothesis about your manager, i.e., they are not doing so good in their mental health because they haven't got knowledge of the 'hands up and breathe' method or how to question/answer their thoughts.

How does it feel when you believe this alternative hypothesis about your manager? Any better?

In my experience, to believe this about a manager produces a lot less emotions/feelings than believing they are evil. It can even allow some empathy, which can result in a radically different approach with your manager. I am certainly in no way suggesting that you have to start liking or agreeing with their behaviour, but only consider, their behaviour is simply an outward expression of unhealthy emotional coping.

Seeing this allows you to feel more calm and better focus on just doing your work and what is required to solve the problems that you are experiencing. It may be that you still need to make a formal complaint about your manager or take steps to highlight your manager's unhealthy behaviour, but you can go about this more calmly. In smaller organisations or organisations which have a lot of corruption, there may not be so much you can do to highlight a manager's unhealthy behaviour. In some cases, changing positions or companies may be the best solution. If it comes to this, perhaps it is time to consider your trust in the universe in showing you the way? Maybe you are being moved to better?

When considering thoughts about managers from hell, I invite you to consider carefully all your 'should' thoughts. These may look a lot like:

They shouldn't be like that.

They should be different.

They should know better.

They should be supportive and kind.

They should resign.

They shouldn't be in that position.

They should be acting and behaving professionally.

They should be supporting me and giving me clear guidance and instruction.

I would suggest that all of these thoughts can be now considered against the new 'poor mental health' hypothesis. Is it true that this person shouldn't be like that and acting in a different way when they have poor mental health? As suggested earlier, managers sadly aren't screened for mental health skills/knowledge before being hired. When you really see this, a lot of these 'should' statements start to collapse.

Please also read the 'Criminals/evil people' hot topic as you may find some slightly different pointers there which could also be helpful for this topic.

# Self-harm

> '**I hurt myself on the outside to kill the monster on the inside.**'
>
> **~ Unknown**

'Self-harm' is often associated with cutting one's skin with either a razor blade, knife, or another sharp object. It is done in order to bring about relief from one's difficult feelings.

There are other behaviours which we can also use to bring about relief from difficult feelings. Some of these behaviours, when used excessively, can also harm the body. In this sense, these behaviours could also be classed as self-harm behaviours.

Below is a list of some other common self-harm behaviours:

Overeating

Eating unhealthy foods in excess

Bingeing and purging

Undereating

Drinking alcohol to excess

Exercising to excess

Smoking

Engaging in risky sexual behaviours

Skin picking

Hair pulling

Taking/smoking drugs

The key point to make about self-harm is that all self-harm is done for one reason only: To bring about relief from one's difficult feelings. You may have wondered why I didn't say thoughts. We never need relief from thoughts, only the feelings that the thoughts have triggered. If thoughts came with peace/calm, would you be concerned about them?

Let's consider the example of self-harm by cutting off the skin:

If I am feeling really angry or sad inside my body and don't have the skills to be able to change that, a simple method to bring about some instant relief is to pick up a knife or razor blade and make a cut on my skin. When I cut my skin, I will feel pain and see blood. The pain I feel from where the blade cut my skin and the blood I see oozing from the cut is enough to provide a distraction from the thoughts and associated feelings I was experiencing in my body and/or mind. For this reason, I start to feel a little bit better. Furthermore, because I started to feel a bit better, the brain then concludes, 'That worked, I should do that again.' This is how self-harm behaviour gets conditioned as a helpful 'emotional coping' strategy. Unfortunately, the moment the pain from the cut starts to wear off and maybe the blood stops, the distraction from my original thoughts and feelings may be lost, and so I start to experience the difficult feelings again. I will then need to cut again in order to bring about the same relief. And so the vicious cycle begins.

The above example can be applied to any of the self-harm behaviours listed above. The pain from the cut and sight of blood, which acts as the 'distraction' force in the cutting example, is changeable to some other 'distracting' sensation/feeling in the other self-harm behaviours.

Consider for yourself how your self-harm behaviour 'distracts' you from the difficult thoughts and feelings you were experiencing prior to the self-harm behaviour.

So how do we start to break conditioned self-harm behaviour?

As highlighted above, all self-harm behaviour is happening in order to bring about relief from one's difficult feelings, due to not having the skills to deal with difficult feelings in a healthy way. The simple solution, therefore, is to learn how to deal with your emotions in a healthy way.

How do we manage emotions in a healthy way?

Of course, it's hands up and breathe and questioning / answering your thoughts!

Be gentle on yourself in accepting that your conditioned behaviour is likely to continue to happen, certainly in the early stages of learning healthy emotional coping skills. When you catch yourself doing your old self-harm behaviours, remind yourself that you are trying to manage some difficult feelings at that moment and ask yourself if you now have a better way to manage your difficult feelings. The more you return to hands up and breathe and questioning/answering your thoughts, the more you bring an end to the 'monster' (thoughts/emotions) and the need for self-harm behaviours.

# Health anxiety and death

'As a general rule, the less one's sense of life fulfillment, the greater one's death anxiety.'
~ Irvin D. Yalom

When it comes to the hot topic of 'Health Anxiety and Death', there seem to be 5 key sub-topics that link to this. This is not to say there are not other sub-topics that can present with health anxiety and death, but here I have selected 5 of the most commonly presenting ones.

1. Not really living
2. Over-identification with form, i.e., body (flesh and bones) and mind/brain
3. 'Missing you' thinking and fear of this arising with death
4. New mums/dads with a full-time parenting role
5. Illness equals suffering

I will now review each of these 5 sub-topics and the connection that they have to the hot topic of 'Health Anxiety and Death'.

1. From experience, I have found that health anxiety and worry about death arises in people who ironically feel that they are not really living!

So whenever a patient presents with much worry and anxiety about their health and dying, the first thing I usually start to discuss and consider with that patient is whether they feel they are really living, i.e., are they living the life they want to be living? If you think about it, it will make sense that if we were living in a way we didn't want to be living for some time, we might then start to worry about our life passing before our eyes and that we die before we ever really get to live. Alternatively, you can consider, when you are really loving your life, are you worrying about your health or death?

Worry and anxiety about health and dying therefore can be a great blessing, an 'alarm bell' to wake us up to where we may need to make some changes in our life or take some small steps to bring about change.

2. I have also found from experience that health anxiety and worry/fear about death can indicate an over-identification with form, i.e., an over-identification with body (flesh and bones) and brain/mind. It can be common for someone that has relied on their looks or body in life, for example, a model or athlete, to experience much anxiety and worry about their body or looks declining or fading.

For these people, they may have learned that 'feeling good' can only be possible when their body or looks are 'perfect'. Likewise, a professor who has relied upon his brain/mind for his career may have learned that 'feeling good' can only be possible when his brain/mind is working good, and so if there is any indication of decline in brain/mind, then much anxiety and worry can start to occur.

How to help this?

Once people have been introduced to the 'hands up and breathe' method, they can start to hands up and breathe to any anxiety related to the subject of death. When people start to see that their anxiety diffuses if they apply the 'hands up and breathe' method, and furthermore that they can produce peace/calm without having to do anything with their looks, body, or mind/brain, the over-identification conditioning with form starts to fall away. People become more whole humans, with recognition of their deeper peaceful essence, which they had not been seeing. The subject of death becomes easier to bear with some ability to connect to peace/calm. I am reminded of the quote by Byron Katie, who says, 'The worst thing that can happen on your deathbed is a belief. Nothing worse than that has ever happened, ever.' Katie is highlighting that a belief – and the associated emotions that arise when thoughts are believed – is the worst that can happen on a deathbed. When emotions diffuse, what's left? Just peace and a body that is shutting down.

3. The third thing to consider with health anxiety and death is the thinking of 'missing' someone. This has actually been presented as a separate hot topic (Missing you) because it is such a common topic to present in my therapy room. As highlighted in that hot topic, 'missing you' thinking is considered a romantic and nice way to think in most societies, and so this allows it to go unquestioned and continue to survive. So long as 'missing' thinking survives, sadness also arises. If someone has experienced this great sadness that arises with the missing thought, they can then start to worry about having to endure this great sadness again every time someone dies or leaves them, which can make them very anxious about death. This can also be projected onto children, for example: 'Because I have such a difficult time with death, my children will also have a very difficult time if I was to die.' This can then make us very anxious about dying and increase health anxiety because we do not want our children to ever have to experience such mental distress.

4. I have worked with many new mums and some dads caring full-time for a newborn child who reported really

bad health anxiety and fear of dying. With further exploration, there seems to be an understandable loss of identity which occurs when a new mum or dad takes on the role of full-time carer for baby, i.e., they lose themselves completely in the many tasks of being a Mum or Dad and maybe start to forget about what used to make them happy. As a result, they may then start to feel that they aren't really living, which can make them anxious about dying, as highlighted earlier (point number 1).

The worry/anxiety can also switch focus slightly to that of how the baby would cope if Mum or Dad dies because they are such a prominent figure in the baby's life. Thoughts such as: 'If I died, what would happen to my baby?' and 'My baby wouldn't survive if I wasn't around.' These thoughts can be quite easily answered and questioned when you apply the 'questioning/answering your thoughts' methods.

Interestingly, health anxiety can also switch from worry/anxiety about a parent's own health to worry/anxiety about their baby's health. The reason for this is often because the full-time carer parent has lost so much of their identity, a worry can then start to arise about how they would ever be able to live a meaningful life again if they weren't a parent. In some patients, I have found both this worry/anxiety and the totally contrasting worry/anxiety about not really living now that they are a parent. This shows how confused the mind can get at times.

In summary, the 3 types of thoughts that can arise in new full-time carer parents are:

- I'm not really living, and so I don't want to die yet.
- How will my child cope if I'm not around anymore? /They wouldn't be able to cope without me.
- How would I cope if my child was not around anymore? /I wouldn't ever be able to have a meaningful life again if my child wasn't around.

5. The final sub-topic in health anxiety and death is the learned belief 'Ill health equals suffering.' Society teaches us from a young age that good health is associated with happiness/feeling good and that ill health is a depressing subject and associated with suffering and distress. It is still quite rare for people to talk about ageing and death in our society, and so the subject remains taboo and a bit mysterious. Something I propose to all of my patients is that it is absolutely possible to be sick and/or even dying yet feel peace and good feeling. I never ask my patients to believe me but to consider what I'm saying and start to experiment with this idea when they experience times of ill health. How to experiment with this? Apply the 'hands up and breathe' skill on any emotions/feelings arising

when ill health is occurring and start to discover that when emotions diffuse, peace becomes clear again. It may be that some physical pain does not diffuse, but peace can be felt in other parts of the body, which makes the pain much easier to bear. An example of this was an 85-year-old lady I worked with who reported constant pain from her hips down (basically all of her legs, lower back, and hips were in pain) from slipped discs in her lower back. When I started working with this lady, she reported much pain and distress. She was visibly frustrated, angry, depressed, and tearful most of the time and regularly wished she was dead. When the lady was introduced to the 'hands up and breathe' skill, she was able to see how it was possible to diffuse her emotions and reconnect to the peace beneath emotions, even though she was experiencing great pain from her hips down. This was the best evidence needed to restructure her belief that she would 'always suffer and live a miserable life so long as she had pain'. The more the lady applied hands up and breathing throughout the day, the more peace the lady started to feel. The lady also reappraised some other beliefs with her new questioning and answering of thoughts skill, which prevented some emotions from returning again. The lady was so grateful and happy to discover that even though the pain from her hips down remained, she was able to feel peace/calm in all the other parts of her body. Furthermore, she was no longer in distress/suffering and was not worrying about death/health anymore. The lady started to do more of the things she wanted to be doing in her life and reported feeling by the end of therapy sessions that she was experiencing more happiness and peace than she had ever experienced in her whole 85 years of life, even with continuing pain from the hips down.

# Worst shame and forgiving self

*'Wherever you find shame, you will find a should thought directed toward yourself.'*
~ K.Snaith

Most of us, at some point in our life, will do something which we really regret. We may regret it so much that we feel we can never tell a single soul about it and must keep it a secret for the rest of our life! We may punish ourselves on a daily basis, for weeks, months, even years in some cases!

Shame is a powerful emotion and can also come with physical symptoms of tension and pain. I have found from experience that shame and our unhealthy attempt to deal with this, i.e., pushing it away and avoiding it, serves to maintain unhealthy emotional coping mechanisms, and so until our 'worst shame' is addressed and dealt with, we are susceptible to future mental health problems.

I have found from experience that it can take several sessions of building up strong trust and rapport with a patient before they feel able to open up about their worst shame. I have found from experience that when someone does open up about their worst shame and reappraise the associated thoughts around this, they can quite drastically improve in mood and report feeling much peace and happiness. I'm also reassured that they are much less likely to experience mental health problems in the future, having addressed a key source of emotional avoidance.

If you are reading this book, the good news is that you don't need to wait to see a therapist or counselor and then another several weeks of building trust/rapport with your therapist/counselor. You can start to confront your worst shame with the new skills you have been introduced to in this book.

How to do it:

The first step, as always, is to hands up and breathe with the shame emotion. Allow the shame fire to peak and fall. Fully allow the shame emotion to do its thing until the shame fire diffuses. This may take several minutes. Once the shame fire is diffused, try to identify what was running through your mind in relation to the shame emotion. I would usually prompt someone to consider what their 'should' thought is. For example:

I should not have done…

I should have done...

Maybe you can also identify some negative/criticising thoughts about yourself. For example:

I'm stupid.

I'm such an idiot.

I'm pathetic.

I'm weak.

Any thoughts identified should be written down on a bit of paper.

When it comes to working the 'should' thought, which is at the heart of the shame emotion, a question I always ask is, 'Why did you do what you did?'

Note down your answer to this question. Sit with the answer you gave, take a few breaths with it, and see that you did what you did because of the answer you gave. Is that a good enough reason why you did what you did? If it isn't good enough, why didn't you do it another way?

What I am inviting people to consider here is that it is pointless saying we should have acted in another way when we didn't act in another way. There was a reason why we didn't act in another way; what was it? Often, with great shame scenarios, we have acted out of an emotional state and then really regret it. I invite people to consider if they knew and applied the 'hands up and breathe' skill at the time. Also, were they questioning their statements and answering their questions in that moment?

When we start to consider that we had little choice in doing what we did because we were in an emotional state and weren't applying skills to change that emotional state, we start to find some forgiveness for ourselves. Still, some self-punishment can come from thinking that we should have learnt a way of dealing with our emotions sooner. Maybe another 'should' thought such as 'I should have learned how to deal with my emotions sooner' may surface.

Consider carefully if that is a really accurate and true statement. Can you consider that our society and parents on the whole do not teach us the 'hands up and breathe' method or healthy ways to manage our emotions, only unhealthy ways? When you see this, this 'should' statement cannot hold up and starts to crumble.

The end of your shoulds is the end of your shame. Please take your time to do the required work on your worst shame so that you can then get on with having good mental health for the rest of your life. Hopefully, you can consider from what has been presented in this hot topic, a therapist or counsellor is never needed to work on your worst shame. You have everything required to do this yourself. However, there is no harm in seeking additional support from a therapist or counsellor if you feel it necessary.

# Evil people and criminals

> 'Forgive them, for they do not know what they are doing'
> ~ Jesus

American psychotherapist and teacher Byron Katie says, 'No one would harm another human being unless they were confused.' I'm inclined to very much agree with Katie. Having worked with many hundreds of patients over the past 5 years, including quite a few ex-prisoners, I've not yet found an evil person. Some may argue that I just need to go to a high security prison for people who have committed horrific crimes, there I will find lots of evil people. I can't comment about that because I haven't been to a high security prison for people who have committed horrific crimes, but I do know that a very confused mind is capable of committing horrific crimes. I have explored this in great detail with the ex-criminals I have worked with.

I once worked with an ex-prisoner who had served years in prison for raping his on and off partner one night in a fit of anger. After talking about what had happened over several hours of sessions, we were able to identify a key thought which was playing in his mind before he did what he did. The thinking playing in his mind before committing the crime was 'She has made me feel powerless and so much pain' and so, 'I want her to feel how I feel.' His partner had quite recently cheated on him with a friend of his, which is why he was feeling a lot of pain and powerless.

After some very gentle questioning of the thought that 'she made me feel powerless and pain', my patient was able to see this simply wasn't true and could never be true for him or anyone. Nobody injects us with feelings/emotions; only our mind is capable of injecting emotions into the body when it believes a thought that isn't true. In that moment of absolute confusion, there is potential to commit great crimes. It's important to note that my patient was also heavily under the influence of alcohol at the time (had a drinking problem) and had been experiencing quite severe mental health problems for some time. This cocktail of factors all came together in that moment, which resulted in a terrible crime being committed.

My patient was able to see clearly that if he had the capacity in that moment to not believe that his partner was making him feel emotions and that his own mind was the only thing that could ever be responsible for that, he wouldn't have acted in the way he acted and committed the crime he did. It was clear from talking that my patient was not equipped with the 'hands up and breathe' skill or the 'questioning/answering your thoughts' skill at the time of the crime. My patient was using a very common 'emotional coping' strategy of drinking alcohol, which is what his parents had taught him as a child. He had never learned how to manage his emotions in a healthy way.

When I worked with my patient, he had been out of prison for about 20 years after serving some years behind bars. Now a 'free man', yet he was still very much in prison on the inside, experiencing daily flashbacks, shame/guilt, anxiety, panic, and other emotions since committing the crime. When finishing sessions with me, the man had started to find forgiveness for himself having seen through some of the untrue thinking he had been carrying for over 20 years. He also felt for the first time that he had really understood 'why' he committed the crime he did and was reassured because of this that he would never act in the same way again. This is true rehabilitation. This man was a classic example of how 'serving time' in prison doesn't help one to really understand and change their behaviour. The man's main way of reassuring himself that he would never commit such a horrible crime again prior to our sessions was to never drink alcohol again. Fortunately, this had worked to keep him out of any more crime, but now he felt truly rehabilitated.

I hope this example highlights the point that a very confused mind is capable of committing horrific acts/crimes. As always, I'm not asking you to believe me but to consider this for yourself, talk to people that have committed great crimes, and try to really understand their perspective before labelling someone as 'evil'.

As mentioned in the 'Managers from hell' hot topic, I have found from experience that labelling people as 'evil' really isn't helpful. Your heart and mind close when you label someone as this, and you no longer feel any peace. I always invite people to consider the quote from Jesus in relation to this topic once it has been properly introduced, 'Forgive them, for they do not know what they are doing.' Can you see how this is true when considering the example of my ex-prisoner patient above?

I hope that this information may one day reach the powers that be within the criminal justice systems so that true rehabilitative change can start to occur within criminal justice systems, rather than just punishment.

# I can't trust anyone

*'I trust everyone to be as they are.'*
*~ K.Snaith*

A very common topic to occur is that of 'trust'. When I have worked with patients who reported much 'let down', 'disappointment' and/or 'betrayal' in their life, it's not at all uncommon for thinking to start to form about not being able to trust anyone. I have found that the thought 'I don't trust anyone' is a very 'sweeping statement' and quite unhelpful thought to live with. How does it make you feel and live when you believe the thought 'I don't trust anyone'?

Do you notice how your heart closes, your defences come up, and maybe you don't talk to people so openly and as much? How does that serve you?

I have found from experience that this thinking only serves in jeopardising good friendships and relationships and leading people to feel more lonely, isolated, and unhappy.

I usually propose to my patients that have this thought a radically different thought. What if we turned it around to 'I trust everyone' but with the added proviso, 'to be as they are'. Let me explain further what I mean by this.

I'm proposing initially that it may be possible to live without any expectations of people until we are able to see how they are, i.e., not to conclude someone is punctual or even that they are bad at timekeeping, but to trust only the evidence you have gained so far. So if when meeting a new friend for the first time they are late, I will note that they are 'late' and maybe that's what I can trust about them for the future. I will also note that it's only one time this has happened, and it may just be a 'freak' exception, but if it happens a second time also, I may more firmly start to conclude that I can trust this person will be late when meeting me. Thinking this way allows me to not feel let down or frustrated/angry when they turn up late to an appointment we have agreed because I was already expecting them to be 'as they are' – late for appointments. Until I have new evidence that they can turn up to appointments (more than one) on time, I am not going to believe that they can do this. This hot topic very much links to the hot topics 'Let down' and 'I'm sorry' and so I would encourage you to also read these topics if you are reading this one.

A common worry expressed at the proposal of thinking 'I trust everyone to be as they are' is that you will somehow be more vulnerable and at risk of harm. I invite you to consider carefully if this would be the case.

I'm not proposing at all that you should trust everyone to always be good and honest, only to be 'as they are', which may actually be quite horrible and dishonest. Seeing people 'as they are' allows for you to be clear about any actions you need to take in order to better protect yourself. Let's consider the example already introduced of the friend turning up late: If I'm trusting them to be 'as they are', which so far is indicating 'late', I can then make plans to do something whilst waiting for them to turn up to our meeting or simply turn up late myself, protecting and making better use of my time.

Experiment with trusting people to be 'as they are' and see how this works for you.

# Let down

> 'People can't let you down, only your belief about people can.'
> ~ K.Snaith

It's highly likely that each and every one of us will experience the feeling of being really let down by someone at some point in our lives. For some of us, this may be a regular occurrence. When this happens, we are likely to experience strong emotions, most probably sadness and/or anger. We will then have to manage these emotions the best we can. A very common emotional coping mechanism I have found from experience when people have been let down is that of sharing our frustrations with others. We will often rant about our being let down to friends or family, and this can be somewhat soothing/therapeutic, particularly when we feel heard and validated. Most friends and family haven't been trained in hands up and breathing or questioning/answering your thoughts skills, and so they often will just agree with us, which may provide some relief from our emotions in the moment. Later, when we are alone and start thinking again about the person who let us down, we are likely to feel all the same emotions because the thoughts causing the emotions have not changed, they have only been validated by friends/family to be reasonable and true.

When considering this hot topic with my patients, I usually tell a very simple story about me meeting a friend for coffee. This story, to some, may seem so trivial and irrelevant to their 'bigger' let down that they may instantly dismiss this example as silly and pointless. If this happens, I invite you to carefully consider the key points of the story and how these could be applied to your 'bigger' let down. I am in no way suggesting this is a big 'let down', but it simply highlights the points I need to make.

The story of me meeting my friend for Coffee:

It's Sunday morning, and my good friend messages me to see if I would like to have a coffee and catch up in the afternoon. I consider carefully, 'Would I like to have a coffee this afternoon?' to which my answer is yes. I consider carefully if I would like to catch up with my friend this afternoon, and my answer is also yes. So I message my friend back agreeing to meet at 2 pm in my favourite organic local coffee shop.

At 1:45 pm, I start driving to my coffee shop, and at 1:59 pm, I pull up just outside the coffee shop. As I'm walking into the coffee shop, I wonder if my friend will be there. I am not expecting my friend to be there, even though we agreed 2 pm. My only thought at this point is, 'I wonder if he will be in there yet.' On entering the coffee shop, I notice he is not there, and so I sit down on a table I like the look of. I check my phone, and he hasn't messaged, and so I have the thought that 'maybe he is on his way as I haven't heard anything'. At this point, I still am not expecting my friend to arrive even though we agreed to meet at 2 pm. I message my friend on WhatsApp just to let him know that I arrived in the coffee shop and have sat down. I'm feeling so happy at this point to be in my favourite coffee shop, looking around at who is there. I smile and say hi to the lovely staff I know from visiting the shop so regularly. I consider the menu and what coffee I would like to drink whilst waiting for my friend to arrive. Five minutes pass, and my friend still has not arrived. I look at my phone to see if he has read my message, and I see that he hasn't; in fact, it says he hasn't been online since this morning after our messaging. I decide at this point that I will now order my favourite coffee (coconut latte) as I'm ready to order, and it is now past the time we said we were meeting. I'm feeling a slight sense of excitement at this point to be waiting for my favourite coffee. I do love my coffee! I continue to look around at the people in the coffee shop whilst noticing the beautiful smell of freshly brewed coffee. Within a few minutes, my coffee arrives. I'm so happy about this. I am delighted to see the beautiful love heart art on the top of my latte and notice the pride the waitress had in placing the coffee on the table in front of me so I could clearly see the love heart art on the top of it. I thank the waitress.

It's now 2:15 pm, and still, my friend hasn't arrived. I notice my message in WhatsApp still hasn't been read, and my friend still isn't showing that he has been online since our chatting this morning. I decide to give my friend a quick ring. I call my friend, but there is no answer. I think it is strange as normally my friend is very reliable in turning up when we arrange to meet so wonder if my friend is okay. I decide that I will try to call again in ten minutes, but in the meantime, I'm just going to really enjoy drinking my latte and catching up on some social media on my phone. Ten minutes pass, and I am having such a lovely time drinking my coffee and catching up on social media. My friend still hasn't arrived, and so I ring him again. Still no answer, but this time I leave a message saying, 'Hey, hope everything is okay, I'm just in the coffee shop, but you haven't arrived yet, give me a buzz to let me know what's happening.' I have the thought that 'I hope my friend is okay', but then have the thought 'I'm just going to make the most of my time by myself in this coffee shop to do what I want as it so rare these days.' And so I do just that, really enjoy finishing off the rest of my coffee whilst doing some more catching up on social media. I also read some emails that I had been wanting to read properly but haven't had time to do so in the last few days. I notice the time, and it's now 3:45 pm. I haven't felt at all let down or disappointed about my friend not coming because as yet, I still haven't believed that he was going to be there, even though we arranged to meet at 2 pm. I've had such a lovely time drinking coffee and catching up on social media and emails in my favourite coffee house. My thoughts then turn back to my friend, and I notice he still hasn't been on WhatsApp and hasn't returned my calls. I consider if there is anything else I can do but decide at the moment there is not, so I will now leave and get on with the rest of my day. I want to get to the supermarket before it shuts at 4 pm, so I hurriedly pay my bill, thank the waitress again, say goodbye, and head to the supermarket feeling really happy. I enjoy the rest of the afternoon.

The end.

What I'd like you to consider from this story is that at no point did my friend have the power to make me feel let down. Only if I believe the thought that my friend 'should be there' can I feel let down. In reality, he clearly shouldn't be there (for whatever reason) as he isn't. When my mind is clear about this, no problem. When my mind is confused about this, i.e., starts to believe that he should be there, that's when I start to experience emotions and a problem.

What to do:

Question any statements about what you think 'should' or 'shouldn't' be happening if you are feeling let down.

Some common feedback I get about this example is that maybe I'm a bit of pushover for not getting angry and annoyed at my friend. One thing I explain is that it would be quite crazy for me to get angry at my friend when for all I know he could be in the intensive care ward on life support machines in the local hospital having had a horrific road traffic accident on the way to the coffee shop. I can't be angry at him until I have gained more information about what's happened. Even then, if anger arose, I'd own it, examine what I was believing in that moment, and question/answer the associated thoughts.

If your goal like mine is to have as much peace as possible, you may want to start owning your 'let downs'. See how it works for you to apply the above pointers when you feel any let down.

# I'm sorry

> 'Sorry is a lovely word to say but meaningless unless we understand the thinking and emotions that caused the behaviour.'
> ~ K.Snaith

This hot topic was put in due to the number of people I have worked with who have suffered repeated abuse at the hands of others due to believing those two words 'I'm sorry'.

When talking to my patients, they all said the same thing to me: 'He/she said sorry and promised me that he/she wouldn't do it again. I believed him/her, so I gave him/her another chance.'

I've come to see that people can be sincerely sorry and offer the most heartfelt apology and assurance that it will never happen again, however, without understanding the thinking and emotions that caused the behaviour, the sorry and promise is actually meaningless. If someone says, 'I won't do that again', I never believe it unless they have expressed real understanding of the thoughts and emotions that caused the behaviour and how they would think differently if a similar or identical scenario arose. Even this wouldn't give me absolute assurance they wouldn't do it again, but it would offer me some good hope of change.

I have worked with many ladies that have been beaten at the hands of their angry husbands only to be told the next morning those words: 'I'm so sorry, I promise I will never do it again.' The ladies all believed those words only to be beaten again some weeks or months later. And so the story continued.

A good example to support this hot topic would be that of the man who raped his girlfriend in the 'Criminals and evil people' hot topic. The man was honest in admitting to me that he had lived for over 20 years since committing his crime with worry and fear that he may 'lose control' again and commit a similar horrific crime. He had managed this constant worry and anxiety by never drinking even a drop of alcohol since committing his crime. After talking for several sessions, the man was able to gain a proper understanding of the thinking that was playing in his mind before he acted to rape his girlfriend. The thinking he had was that 'she has made me feel this way', which, of course, can never be true. Nobody can ever make us feel anything; only our thinking can cause emotions. Truly seeing and understanding this provided the man with great reassurance that he would never act in a similar way again, which he had not felt since the crime. My patient had offered up the words 'I'm sorry, I will never do that again' to various people since committing his crime, in addition to abstaining from alcohol for over 20 years, but only felt sincere about these words after understanding his mind.

If 'I'm sorry' is a key theme in your life (saying it or receiving those words), I invite you to consider the meaningless nature of these words until the mind is really understood. Only when you understand mind (cause) can you bring about change to behaviour (effect).

# Parenting

*'We cannot teach what we do not know ourselves.'*
*~ K.Snaith*

Children are mini-adults. Some people may take issue with this statement, suggesting it isn't true because children's brains and bodies are very different to adults. This may be the case, but psychologically, children experience thoughts and the full spectrum of human emotions in exactly the same way that adults do. Children's thought processes and vocabulary may not be as complex as adults, but like adults, they will experience emotions when untrue thoughts are believed.

Anyone that has ever sat with a child and taken time to understand what a child is thinking can see this to be clearly the case. I once tried to teach English to Chinese children (it didn't go so well, which is why I'm writing this book!) and recall a small Chinese girl getting really angry at Frankie the frog in one lesson (Frankie was a cuddly frog puppet which I bought to help with engaging the children in lesson). When I asked her why she was angry, she clearly expressed to me, 'I'm angry at Frankie because he hasn't spoken to me today!' When

I inquired more about this, it was clear, 'Frankie should speak to me.' Frankie didn't speak because my ventriloquism skills aren't quite polished yet, and so rather than telling her this, I explained to the little girl, 'Frankie is feeling shy today and so only felt that he could speak to me in my ear today.' This seemed to relieve her anger somewhat, but she insisted that next time she wanted Frankie to speak. That's when I resigned from my teaching English to Chinese children job. All joking aside, this girl was 6 years old and clearly expressing thoughts that argue with her 'reality' in exactly the same way adults have thoughts that argue with their reality. When thoughts argue with reality – truth – we experience emotions.

I encourage all parents I have worked with to introduce the 'hands up and breathe' skill and 'questioning/answering your thoughts' skill to children from as early an age as possible. This can be done in really creative ways and even incentivised. For example: A ladder-reward poster system on the wall could be implemented so that each time the child performs hands up and breathing when they experience a strong emotion, they move up the ladder, eventually receiving a reward that is appealing to the child when they have done it a number of times. A similar ladder could be used for questioning / answering your thoughts.

I'd love to hear the creative ways that you come up with to teach these skills to your children. Please also share this information with your friends who also have children.

More peace in the world starts with you and your children!

Another sub-topic to consider in relation to this hot topic is the anger we can often feel towards our own parents for doing a 'bad job' when bringing us up. A simple end to this anger is for you to consider whether your parents had training in and understanding of the 'hands up and breathe' skill and 'questioning/answering your thoughts' skill when they were bringing you up. How can they possibly teach you what they didn't have themselves? The quote, 'Forgive them for they do not know what they are doing' springs to mind, which also links to the hot topics of 'Evil people and criminals' and 'Managers from hell'.

# Jealousy

> *'Jealousy, that dragon which slays love under the pretence of keeping it alive.'*
> ~ H. Havelock Ellis

Jealousy, like 'missing someone', is something that is romanticised in our society. We are taught in society from an early age that it's healthy and good to feel some jealousy in a relationship because it shows that we really love and care for someone. I've come to see this really isn't the case and that jealousy is only ever unquestioned thoughts about attraction, oneself, being alone, and the cause of emotions, which has the potential to really destroy a relationship if left unexamined. The quote 'Jealousy, that dragon which slays love under the pretence of keeping it alive.' (H. Havelock Ellis) sums it up nicely.

Envy, another type of jealousy, can exist outside of intimate relationships. This jealousy type is concerned with people having something that we feel we need/want. Envy may not be such a common word for people to use, and so often, people may just refer to this feeling as 'jealous' and never have considered the difference between the two types of jealousy.

Envy may not be something that is romanticised so much in our society, but because it 'feels' similar and we have learned to not examine the first type of jealousy (the intimate relationship type), we are unlikely to examine this second type also, which allows for its continuing existence.

So let's consider what the first type of jealousy can be made up of. The first type seems to be able to be broken down into 4 key areas with various thoughts and emotions under each:

1. Confusion about attraction:

    THOUGHT: They shouldn't be finding another person attractive.
    EMOTION: Anger

2. Fear of being alone:

    THOUGHT: They are going to leave me.
    EMOTION: Anxiety

    THOUGHT: I will never meet anyone again.
    EMOTION: Sadness

    THOUGHT: I should have seen what he/she was like from the beginning and never got into this relationship.
    EMOTION: Shame

THOUGHT: I can't cope by myself and/or with being single again.
EMOTION: Anxiety/Panic

3. Self-esteem/negative thoughts about self:

    THOUGHT: I'm ugly.
    EMOTION: Sadness

    THOUGHT: I'm too fat.
    EMOTION: Sadness

    THOUGHT: I'm stupid/an idiot.
    EMOTION: Anger/Shame

    THOUGHT: I'm unlovable.
    EMOTION: Sadness

4. Confusion about where emotions come from:

    THOUGHT: They have made me feel this way.
    EMOTION: Anger

Can you recognise any of these thoughts and emotions that arise with Jealousy? This is not an exhaustive list of the thoughts and emotions that can occur with Jealousy but just highlighting some of the common ones I have identified from my work.

As you can see from this, 4 out of the 5 'big 5' emotions could arise with these thoughts, and so that is why 'Jealousy' can be such a powerful and difficult feeling to manage when it surfaces. Jealousy, therefore, isn't one emotion but a collection of emotions.

What happens when you question the truthfulness and accuracy of all these statements? Hopefully, you can see that they start to crumble with some gentle questioning.

Let's now consider each of the 4 points in a bit more detail:

1. Confusion about attraction:

Where did we learn that we should only ever find one person attractive? How realistic is this? I would suggest that it's very unrealistic to consider that you will only ever find one person attractive and a recipe for confusion and distress when you start to notice yourself being attracted to more than one person. There is a difference in finding someone attractive and actually getting into a bed with them and/or starting a relationship with them. I notice on a daily basis that I can be sexually attracted to lots of people, yet I choose to have a monogamous relationship, which I'm very happy in.

2. Fear of being alone:

If we have been in a relationship or many relationships for a long time, we can start to forget how we managed to cope when we were single. As a result, anxiety can start to form around the subject of 'being single', and so this is likely to be activated any time there is a potential threat to our relationship. When I have sat with patients and looked at this anxiety, most people are able to notice that they were okay alone and were doing just fine before they started their relationship. This may not always be the case, and for some people, they may never have really felt 'good' until they were in a relationship. For these people, it's much harder to shake the anxiety about being alone because they don't yet have the evidence that they can feel good being alone. The good news is that after learning the 'hands up and breathe' skill and 'questioning/answering your thoughts' skill, people can start to be convinced that it's possible to bring about their own peace (feeling good) whenever they apply their skills. This offers some evidence that maybe it would be possible to feel good if they weren't in a relationship. Practice, practice, and more practice of the skills is likely to really reduce anxiety about being 'single' or alone.

3. Self-esteem/negative thoughts about self: How you view yourself has a lot to do with how you will react if you consider that your partner may be attracted to or interested in someone else. If you are very comfortable

and at peace with yourself, you are less likely to react if your partner appears to be finding someone else attractive. In contrast, if you have a very low opinion and many critical thoughts about yourself, these are likely to go into 'overdrive' should you start to consider that your partner is finding someone else attractive. Jealousy can therefore very much indicate the presence of low-self esteem or negative thoughts about self. I encourage my patients to write down all of their negative thoughts about self and examine them one by one using the 'questioning/answering your thoughts' skill. Some of the other hot topics may be particularly helpful for this, for example, 'I'm too fat/skinny', 'I'm ugly', and 'I'm stupid'.

4. Confusion about where emotions come from: Pointing the finger at anyone to be the cause of your emotions is crazy. Why do I say this? Quite simply, nobody is walking around with syringes loaded with emotions, injecting emotions into us! Only our mind can inject emotions into the body when thoughts are believed which aren't true. When you consider that someone is causing your emotions, you can get really angry at that person and even want to hurt them. A good example of this was highlighted in the 'Criminals and evil people' hot topic.

Let's now consider envy, the other form of jealousy. Envy seems to be able to be broken down into 3 key areas with various thoughts and emotions under each of these:

1. Over-identification with form:

    THOUGHT: I need that to feel good/happy.
    EMOTION: Sadness

    THOUGHT: I'm going to feel miserable for the rest of my life.
    EMOTION: Anxiety/Sadness

2. Playing God in your life:

    THOUGHT: I want that./It's not fair, I should be having that right now.
    EMOTION: Anger

    THOUGHT: I shouldn't be feeling envious (jealous) of other people.
    EMOTION: Shame/Guilt

3. Confusion about where emotions come from:

    THOUGHT: They have made me feel this way.
    EMOTION: Anger

Can you recognise any of these thoughts and emotions that arise with Envy? Again, this is not an exhaustive list of the thoughts and emotions that can occur with Envy but just highlighting some of the common ones I have identified from my work.

As you can see from this, 4 out of the 5 'big 5' emotions could arise with these thoughts, and so that is why Envy can be such a powerful and difficult feeling to manage when it surfaces. Envy, therefore, isn't one emotion but a collection of emotions.

What happens when you question the truthfulness and accuracy of all these statements? Hopefully, you can see that they start to crumble with some gentle questioning.

Let's now consider each of the 3 points in a bit more detail:

1. Over-identification with form: This subject is also considered in the hot topic about health anxiety and death. In summary, some people have learned that 'feeling good' can only happen with certain things in place, for example, perfect looks and/or body, money in the bank, a relationship, a good career, a mind that is working well, status in society, or fame. If this learning has happened, whenever there is a threat to any of these things or an absence of these things, emotions will be

activated. Learning the 'hands up and breathe' skill for emotions can start to give you quick new evidence that nothing is required to feel good. The more hands up and breathing is practiced when emotions arise, the more the conditioning starts to break away and new learning is formed that 'feeling good' is our nature and never requires anything.

2. Playing God in your life: This is considered in various hot topics and is also very relevant with envy. If we are looking at others and considering how we haven't got that thing we want to have in our life, it's important to consider have we started to play 'God' in our life. I usually ask my patients to consider carefully, 'Are you sure you want to take on the role of God? It's a big job.' This question can instantly make us more humble to consider that maybe it's just not meant to be for us right now because other things are more important, or there are steps required before we get that thing we really want. We can sometimes ironically also shame ourselves for feeling envious towards others as we have also learned that it's not so nice to be envious of others. Interestingly, this is just another form of 'playing God'. We are now dictating that we 'should be more evolved psychologically' than we are. I invite people to consider that we can only be as evolved psychologically as we are in any moment, until we take the necessary learning to evolve. To suggest that

we should be ahead of our time is to 'play God' once again. Considering this is often enough to break this thinking. It's also good to consider here whether we have had access to the 'hands up and breathe' skill and 'questioning/answering your thoughts' skill to help us evolve psychologically. Seeing that you can't evolve without the right skills to evolve can help you to be more forgiving to yourself if you are 'envying others'.

3. Confusion about where emotions come from: As already pointed out earlier, pointing the finger at anyone to be the cause of your emotions is crazy. Only your mind can inject emotions into your body when it believes thoughts that aren't true.

# Diet and exercise

*'The doctor of the future will give no medicine, but will instruct his patient in the care of the human frame, in diet and in the cause and prevention of disease.'*
*- Thomas A. Edison.*

Some may wonder why I'm including a hot topic about diet and exercise in a book about mental health. The simple answer to this is that the body and mind are not able to be separated; one always influences the other. If your goal is to achieve good mental health, then you have to consider the health of your body, which is very much influenced by diet and exercise.

I have found when working with patients over the years that a vicious cycle can exist with diet and exercise when mental health problems arise. When we experience depression and/or anxiety disorders, we can start to lose focus on eating healthily and exercising because we are so focussed on just trying to 'feel' better in our mental health. Unfortunately, as pointed out above, the body and mind are inseparable, and so if our physical health and fitness start to decline because we are not putting any focus on this, our mental health is likely to be also affected as a consequence. A simple example to highlight this would be someone putting on lots of weight because they stop exercising and eating a balanced and healthy diet as a result of feeling very depressed and putting all their energy and focus into trying to recover from their depression (even if ineffective methods such as rumination/worrying are employed). This person with added bodyweight and decreased fitness may then start to find daily chores and other tasks a lot more difficult to complete. They may require more time and rest to complete their usual chores/tasks, which means less time overall to get things done. As a consequence, daily chores and tasks may then start to build up, adding further stress to their situation. Equally, more bodyweight and less fitness may cause an increase in self-critical or negative thoughts about self, which only further exacerbates low mood and anxiety. The person may feel so 'ugly' and/or 'useless' with their added body weight and lack of fitness that they start to consider nobody would be interested in them anymore, and so they start to withdraw from friends and family. This then causes the person to feel isolated and lonely, which further adds to the emotions 'hot-pot'. And so the vicious cycle continues...

What to do:

I have found from experience that simply highlighting the above vicious cycle can help people to be a little more gentle on themselves when it comes to diet and exercise. Once this is understood, I then invite people to start to consider the importance of 'planning' with diet and exercise. This may seem very obvious, but mental health problems breed bad habits and a forgetting of this simple truth.

I always use the following quote to get people thinking about planning:

'Failing to plan is planning to fail.' ~ Alan Lakein

I invite people to consider what happens if they leave for a day of work without any prior planning as to what they will eat that day. The usual answer is that they end up eating fast-food and/or junk-food because it's the quickest and maybe only option open to them in their work environment. I then get people to consider what would happen if they spent just a couple of minutes planning the night before they go to work or even in the morning before they head off for work. The answer is usually very different. Often people will report that if they had considered it for a few minutes, they would have prepared a quick healthy packed lunch and snacks to take to work. Alternatively, they may decide with a few minutes planning that they will drop by a healthy food cafe/shop on their way to work to pick up something for their lunch.

The same is true for exercise. If we do not spend a couple of minutes planning exactly when we will fit in some exercise for the day, we are likely to get swept along by our busy day and end up not doing any exercise that day.

In summary, if exercise and diet seem like an important topic for you, please consider the inseparable connection between body and mind and the vicious cycle that can occur between mental health problems and diet and exercise. Spend a few minutes planning exactly what you are going to eat each day and exactly when you will exercise each day, and it will happen. Test this out for yourself and see how it works for you.

# I'm stupid

'You can't know something that you haven't learned yet.'

~ K.Snaith

A very common worry reported in my clinic room is the worry about being perceived as 'stupid'. I really love working with this worry because I have found from experience that it can't hold up to more than 10 minutes of discussion and/or questioning.

To help with this worry, I usually play a little game with people, the game of 'ask me something that you think I won't know the answer to'. Here is how it works:

I invite my patient to consider carefully something they think I won't know the answer to. It can be literally anything, but this exercise can work better if it is something skill-related, i.e., maybe something they do in their life, which requires some specific or specialist knowledge. For example, they could ask me, 'What does an ECG (in healthcare) tell you?' or 'What are cc's on a motorbike?'

I will then usually answer my patient with 'I don't know the answer to that.' (Often, there is much laughter involved in this game as I have had some corker questions!) I then ask my patient, 'Tell me honestly now, do you think I'm stupid?' I've never had a patient answer yes to this question. I then ask why they don't think I'm stupid. The standard answer I get back is, 'Because you wouldn't know that because you don't do that type of work or need to have that knowledge in your day to day life.' I agree wholeheartedly with my patient at this point. I then swap roles and ask my patient a question I don't think they will know the answer to. Usually, I will ask them something psychology or biology related as they are my two areas of specialism. I have always been able to find a question that my patient does not know the answer to. I then express to my patient that I don't think they are stupid for not knowing the answer to my question because I never expected them to know the answer as it's not knowledge they would have come across or be using in their day-to-day life.

I then change the game slightly to imagine that we have two famous people in the room with us. I usually make one of the famous people Joey Essex, a celebrity who is often 'mocked' for being 'stupid'. I highlight that as a 'socialite' and someone that just turns up to parties and nightclubs every day, Joey may have no need to know where 'Africa' is or even who the current UK Prime Minister is. I advise, however, that I am very confident even Joey Essex would be able to play this game and ask us something that we didn't know the answer to, even if it was just 'What are the ingredients in a 'sex on the beach' cocktail?' I then use Einstein as my second famous person in the room with us (he has come back from the dead) because he is someone considered to be highly intelligent. I highlight that even someone as intelligent as Einstein can be found to not know something if it's outside his day to day skills and knowledge.

This little game highlights nicely how we all have specialist knowledge depending on what we do in our day to day life and that we can never be stupid for not knowing something that we have never learned.

It's important to be clear about our definition of the word 'stupid'. I have found from experience that most people have never really considered what the word actually means when they are throwing it about to insult someone. The dictionary definition of 'stupid' I find does not always fit the implied meaning of the word. A more accurate meaning/definition of the word 'stupid' that I have been able to develop with patients is:

You should know something that you haven't learned yet.

When we say it like that, it almost sounds a little bit crazy, right?

I usually advise patients that I never worry about anyone accusing me of being 'stupid' because I have a great comeback line for the accuser, i.e., 'It sounds like you think I should know something that I don't know, is that right?' Can you imagine your accuser's reaction when you calmly respond with this question? Hopefully, even a super angry accuser would be able to see with this question the impossibility of their remark.

# Sleep

*'If you want to sleep well, you have to follow some simple rules.'*
~ K.Snaith

When it comes to getting a good night's sleep, it seems that certain rules have to be followed. I have developed a set of rules from working with many hundreds of people experiencing sleep problems over the years. It seems that mental health problems often go hand in hand with sleep problems and that in most cases, the mental health problem may have caused the sleep problem to develop as a result of bad habits forming. The first and foremost thing to do to help with sleep problems is therefore to work on improving your mental health. This requires you making regular time each day for the 'hands up and breathe' skill and also the 'questioning/answering your thoughts' skill. I have found from experience that as mental health improves, sleep problems also start to improve, often without having to put any focus on sleep. In some cases, more focussed work on sleep is required, and so it may then be helpful to consider the following sleep rules.

## SLEEP RULES:

1. Aim to get to bed within the same 3-hour window each night. For example, if your usual sleep time is midnight, then your 3-hour window would be 11 pm – 1 am. Try not to go to bed outside of this window.

2. Aim to wake within the same 3-hour window each morning. For example, if your usual wake time is 8 am, then your 3-hour window would be 7 am – 9 am. Try not to get up outside of this window.

3. Protect sleep time for sleeping and do not do anything else in this time. This includes: eating, writing, watching tv, playing on your phone, playing computer games, cleaning, cooking, etc.

4. Do not drink any caffeinated drinks for at least 4 hours (ideally 6) before bed.

5. Ensure that the room is a comfortable temperature and that you are protected from anything that is likely to interrupt or disturb your sleep as much as possible.

6. Do not eat for at least 3 hours before you sleep.

7. Do not drink for at least 1 hour before you sleep.

8. Ensure your mattress is comfortable and you have appropriate bedding/pillows to support a comfortable position when sleeping.

9. Turn off all electrical equipment, including mobile phones ideally before sleeping. For some, this may be quite anxiety-provoking and require further exploration of thoughts.

10. If you take a nap in the day time, set an alarm so that you don't sleep for more than 30 minutes.

11. Do not take a nap for at least 6 hours before bed.

12. If your mind is racing at night and can't stop worrying, this most probably indicates that you are not making enough time for your mental health skills ('hands up and breathe' and 'questioning/answering your thoughts') in the day time before you go to sleep, which is why worry is coming out at night. Schedule in daily time for your mental health skills. To manage this situation when it is happening, the best strategy may be the 'hands up and breathe' skill on the emotion/s which the worry is unsuccessfully attempting to manage. If after doing hands up and breathing fully on the emotion/s, the mind still seems very unsettled/worried, it may be worth turning the light on and getting some thoughts down on a bit of paper for five minutes or so. I only recommend doing this

if hands up and breathing has not been sufficient in calming the emotions and mind. It may be that the worry is related to 'remembering to do something', in which case, hands up and breathing won't help with this. Writing a note or messaging/emailing yourself so it is visible in the morning will be a much better strategy for settling the mind in relation to this. If you find that this is happening too regularly, it may point towards you needing to make more time for reviewing your day before you go to sleep.

13. As noted in point 12: Always make time to review the day before you go to bed (ideally at the end of your working day) so that you can make a note of any outstanding tasks or things you need to do tomorrow or in the future. This will best ensure you don't start thinking about this at night.

14. If you are experiencing nightmares at night which are waking you up, it may be worth making a quick note on some paper (you can keep a little notepad by the side of the bed) about the nightmare when you wake up so that you can review your thoughts about this in the daytime. Nightmares can indicate unexamined thoughts. It's best to examine thoughts in the day time when you are fully awake. Reappraising thoughts in the day time can help stop the nightmares occurring at night.

15. Fear of death can be a factor in sleep problems, particularly when falling asleep, but it can also come out in nightmares. Please refer to the hot topic on 'health anxiety and death' to help address this.

16. Over-reliance on sleep medication can be a factor in sleep problems. Practicing your mental health skills daily whilst trying to adhere to all of these sleep rules will help you to break an over-reliance on sleep medication. You may need to put some focus on specific worries related to 'coming off medication'. Remember that thoughts are best examined in the day time when you are fully awake.

17. When first attempting to improve your sleep, you may notice that you are waking up a few times in the night. This rhythm may have been established due to bad habits forming in the past. I strongly encourage you to not leave the bed but just see the waking times as opportunities to rest and relax. Even if you are not sleeping, rest and relaxation is really helpful and will ensure you cope better for the next day. You can use the 'hands up and breathe' skill on any emotions that come in when you wake up. Frustration emotion may be a common one to arise when waking up. Reminding yourself of the reappraisal 'I should be waking up because of old bad habits that may have been established' may help to settle any frustration (anger) emotion.

# Career

> 'Forget the money, because, if you say that getting the money is the most important thing, you will spend your life completely wasting your time. You'll be doing things you don't like doing in order to go on living, that is to go on doing things you don't like doing, which is stupid.'
> ~ Alan Watts

Career is one of the most commonly presented topics in my therapy room. This topic can be particularly relevant for younger adults just starting their careers but also for people that have trained in a particular career, only to then find it is not making them happy as they had imagined it would.

When it comes to career, I almost always will refer to a short clip on YouTube called 'What if money was no object?' This short clip contains an audio of Alan Watts speaking. Alan Watts was a British philosopher (now deceased). I will play this audio clip to my patients and let them consider his words. I feel he says it so simply and beautifully that I can't do any better job to make people reflect on this hot topic.

In summary, Alan Watts is suggesting 'Forget the money, because, if you say that getting the money is the most important thing, you will spend your life completely wasting your time. You'll be doing things you don't like doing in order to go on living, that is to go on doing things you don't like doing, which is stupid.' He has a good point, don't you think?

The most common feedback from patients after listening to the short clip is, 'Yes, I do understand and agree with it, but I also have to be realistic and pay the bills!'

I wholeheartedly agree with my patients whenever this feedback is offered, and I'm sure Alan Watts would also agree with this if he was still alive. However, perhaps Alan's undiluted message is a reminder to us all that at the very least, we need to be sowing some seeds into doing something that would really excite us, or we end up living a life doing only what we don't want to be doing in order to pay the bills, which is likely to make us very unfulfilled and unhappy.

Consider the answer to his questions carefully: 'What do you desire? What makes you itch? What sort of a situation would you like?' I encourage my patients to really sit with these questions over a good hour of time, so it is not a rushed exercise.

I have included a transcript of the YouTube short audio clip, just in case you do not have access to the internet to be able to listen.

The link is: https://youtu.be/khOaAHK7efc

TRANSCRIPT OF AUDIO CLIP:

What do you desire? What makes you itch? What sort of a situation would you like? Let's suppose, I do this often in vocational guidance of students, they come to me and say, well, 'We're getting out of college, and we have the faintest idea what we want to do.' So I always ask the question, 'What would you like to do if money were no object? How would you really enjoy spending your life?' Well, it's so amazing as a result of our kind of educational system, crowds of students say, well, we'd like to be painters, we'd like to be poets, we'd like to be writers, but as everybody knows, you can't earn any money that way. Or another person says, well, 'I'd like to live an out-of-doors life and ride horses.' I said, 'You want to teach in a riding school? Let's go through with it. What do you want to do?' When we finally got down to something, which the individual says he really wants to do, I will say to him, 'You do that and forget the money, because, if you say that getting the money is the most important thing, you will spend your life completely wasting your time. You'll be doing things you don't like doing in order to go on living, that is to go on doing things you don't like doing, which is stupid. Better to have a short life that is full of what you like doing than a long life spent in a miserable way. And after all, if you do really like what you're doing, it doesn't matter what it is, you can eventually turn it – you could eventually become a master of it. It's the only way to become a master of something, to be really with it. And then you'll be able to get a good fee for whatever it is. So don't worry too much. That's everybody is – somebody is interested in everything, anything you can be interested in, you will find others will. But it's absolutely stupid to spend your time doing things you don't like in order to go on spending things you don't like, doing things you don't like, and to teach our children to follow in the same track. See, what we are doing is we're bringing up children and educating to live the same sort of lives we are living. In order that they may justify themselves and find satisfaction in life by bringing up their children to bring up their children to do the same thing, so it's all retch and no vomit. It never gets there. And so, therefore, it's so important to consider this question: What do I desire?'

## Pain and sickness

> 'I haven't taken a single painkiller in over ten years. All pain has a message in it. I don't want to kill the message.'
> ~ K.Snaith

Mental health and pain/physical sickness seem to go hand in hand with one influencing the other. Mental health problems can cause us to neglect physical health because we are putting so much focus on 'feeling better' that we lose focus on eating a healthy balanced diet and exercising regularly. Mental health problems can affect our sleep, which can start to impact upon our health. Furthermore, people experiencing mental health problems will often take strong pharmaceutical medications over long periods of time, which can start to impact upon our health. The other side of the equation is what happens mentally when pain/physical sickness arises. Mental resistance to pain/physical sickness/symptoms can cause us to feel distressed, depressed, and hopeless, ultimately contributing to 'unpeace' inside, which serves to confirm the belief that we can't 'feel okay' when we are sick.

Society has supported this belief from an early age, teaching us that sickness and pain are bad things. They are depressing things, things to be gotten 'rid of' as soon as possible. In addition, society teaches us that taking painkillers is a natural, healthy, and even 'responsible' thing to do. As a result, most people have no hesitation in 'popping a painkiller' at the first sign of any pain.

Having worked in physical and mental healthcare for over a decade, I have seen first hand the damage that can occur to physical health as a result of chronic pharmaceutical usage, particularly painkillers and anti-psychotropic medications. Indeed, I was quite shocked to learn that Iatrogenic disease (illness and death caused by the medical system itself, including pharmaceuticals) is the leading cause of death in the United States, above cancer and heart disease.

So it's clear then if we want to have good physical health, we need to stop relying so much on pharmaceuticals and start taking control of our own health, via nutrition, regular exercise, and good sleep in particular.

We need to learn also that all physical symptoms are an indication of 'disharmony' in mind and/or body. Popping a painkiller to 'rid yourself of the pain' is just 'shooting the messenger'. I encourage all of my patients to start taking a 'hands up and breathing' approach to all physical symptoms that arise within the body. This serves to help in three ways: It breaks the 'resistance' to physical symptoms which causes the 'unpeace' feeling, gives us new evidence (peace) to help restructure the belief that we 'can't feel okay with sickness' and allows pain and/or physical symptoms to be 'processed'. How can pain and/or physical symptoms be 'processed' I hear some of you ask? I've come to see that all pain and physical symptoms are moving, just as life is constantly moving. When we hands up and breathe to pain and physical symptoms, we can actually start to witness this movement happening. Often, realisations can happen also with allowing our physical pain and symptoms. I've had many a patient report 'movement' and even complete diffusal/disappearance of pain and/or physical symptoms after doing the 'hands up and breathe' skill. Similarly, many patients have reported a new thought or realisation after doing the 'hands up and breathe' skill, which they hadn't had before.

A very common thought to present when discussing the subject of pain with patients is:

'I'm in pain.'

At first glance, this seems like a totally natural thought for someone to be having that is experiencing pain. I would agree it is a very natural thought to be having if you are experiencing pain; however, I've come to see that it isn't a very balanced, accurate, or helpful thought to be having.

I usually enquire with my patient if the 'whole' of them is in pain, i.e., is every part of their body and head in pain? I've yet to meet a patient that answers yes to this question. I then invite my patient to clarify exactly which part of them is in pain.

They may say, for example: 'My big toe and ankle are experiencing some pain right now, but the rest of me feels fine.'

Compare this to:

'I'm in pain.'

Which seems more accurate and true now that they are both presented?

More importantly, which one feels the best?

Gaining some perspective and focus of where in the body feels good can really help to cope with pain, whereas believing 'I'm in pain' shifts all our focus of attention to the area of pain, which can make it much harder to bear. Experiment with this simple reframe in addition to using the 'hands up and breathe' skill whenever you notice any pain or physical symptoms arising.

# Dating and relationships

> 'If you want to test out how good you have done in working through your self-critical thoughts, go on a date!'
> ~ K.Snaith

The subject of dating and, in particular, how we are often left feeling with dating often presents in my therapy room.

Dating usually brings up 3 sub-topics:

1. How we feel about ourself.
2. How we feel about being single.
3. Unclarity about what we are looking for in a partner.

If we were very comfortable and at peace with ourselves and being single, and had total clarity over what we wanted in a partner, dating would be a breeze!

The reality, though, is that most of us are not comfortable with ourselves and being single and are not clear about what we want in a future partner, and so dating becomes fraught with emotions and confusion!

Let's review each of these 3 sub-areas in turn.

1. Dating brings up lots of self-critical thoughts because it is a time when we are under scrutiny by another. Some people may not like to think of dating like this, but in reality, dating is a time when we have to make conclusions about someone in order to decide if we want to continue getting to know that person or not. Furthermore, it is a time when someone we like could potentially decide that we aren't right for them and let us know this.

If we have 'insecurities' about ourselves, which are basically unexamined thoughts about ourselves, we can naturally worry and be very anxious that a potential date may discover these. Dating, therefore, becomes fraught with anxiety and worry. Some people may try their hardest to 'cover up' their perceived flaws by changing their personality or looks, becoming an inauthentic version of themself. This can be a very confusing scenario as if a date appears to be liking us, we can then naturally worry and be very anxious about how long we can 'keep up the pretense' to our date. Alternatively, if someone lets us know that they don't feel we are a 'match' or maybe more bluntly tells us 'I'm not attracted to you', we can then start to wonder whether they would have been attracted to the more authentic version of ourself. We may then feel quite sad and ruminate over how we will never get to discover the answer to this question.

What to do:

I encourage all my patients to write down everything they dislike about themselves. A slightly different approach to bring out 'dislikes about ourselves' could be to write down everything we wouldn't want people to think about us. The answers to these two different questions are likely to look very similar. The latter question can bring out some concerns about ourselves, which weren't so obvious when we considered the first question.

You could try both approaches and see if one brings out more 'dislikes' than another. Once you have written down your dislikes, try to change them into clear statements about yourself the best you can. Once you have statements, you can use the 'questioning your statements' skill to see if you can come up with a more realistic/accurate thought about yourself. Work each statement, one at a time, until you have covered all the statements on your list. Remember, it is essential to be doing the 'hands up and breathe' skill when working difficult thoughts. New thoughts cannot integrate properly without a good feeling (peace/calm). When you are thinking in a more balanced way about all these statements, your work is done, and you are less likely to worry about someone thinking any of the thoughts you used to think about yourself. Equally, if someone decides you are not right for them, you can just accept they have their reason for this without all of your self-critical thoughts coming into it.

When you have worked through all of your self-critical thoughts, you do not need to 'pretend' to be something that you are not in an attempt to hide your perceived flaws, and so you will never miss the chance to really know if you are a match with someone.

2. This came up also in the hot topic about jealousy. In brief, if we are concerned and not comfortable with being alone, we are more 'needy' of a relationship, and this is likely to make us more anxious when dating because we 'need' someone to like us. This neediness can also cloud our vision of what someone is really like. If we were happy being single and enjoying our life, we are not so needy of a relationship, and so we can just relax about whether someone likes us or not. Furthermore, we are more likely to see someone in an accurate way. It's therefore important when dating to write down all your thoughts about being single. When you have a list of clear statements about being single, you can examine them, one at a time, using the questioning your statements skill.

3. If we are not clear about what we would like in a partner, we can end up pursuing things with people that are just not compatible with us. This wastes our time in finding someone that is compatible with us and can also cause lots of emotions and worry. I'm reminded of the expression, 'If you don't know where you are going, you will end up someplace else.' It's therefore very important that you have clearly considered what you would like in a relationship. This doesn't mean you have to have a rigid checklist of requirements, but when you consider it, there are likely to be some 'big things' or requirements that you are unwilling to budge on. Perhaps an important thing to consider here is a 'compatible vision for the future'. I have found from experience that two people can be very compatible in the present, but if they share very different visions for the future, it may not be feasible for a relationship to happen. Another consideration in relation to this point is how 'lust' and 'sexual attraction' can often sway our 'agenda' of what's really good for us. I'm sure we all have the story of that one person who 'drove us crazy' sexually yet was a nightmare in every other aspect. Gaining some mastery over our sexual desires is therefore of key importance in helping us to find a compatible partner. I recommend using the 'hands up and breathe' skill to gain more control over sexual desires.

Take some time to really consider what you would like your partner to be like and what you can and can't accept in a partner. Maybe write these things down and review them regularly.

If you are experiencing distress and many emotions as a result of dating, please consider carefully all of the above 3 sub-topics and how they may relate to you.

I was considering writing a separate hot topic on relationships, i.e., the next stage after dating, but after careful consideration, I feel that all of the 3 sub-topics highlighted for dating can also be relevant for relationship problems. I, therefore, decided to make dating and relationships one hot topic. I would, however, likely include 3 additional sub-topics when thinking specifically about relationships. These are:

1. Expectations
2. Complacency
3. Accepting people as they are

I will now briefly review each of these:

1. Expectations about how our partner 'should' be can cause many arguments and disharmony in relationships. Expectations can often be driven by unexamined beliefs about love, for example: If they love me, they should know what I want. Expectations can also be driven by a

lack of understanding or appreciating that people have different values and beliefs as a result of their upbringing.

Questioning our expectations or 'should' statements about love and our partner is therefore likely to contribute to much more peace and understanding in the relationship. Equally, it could be that after questioning some expectations, you still feel that you have highlighted a requirement in your relationship that you are unwilling to be flexible on. This can then be discussed calmly and clearly with your partner in order to ascertain if it can be accommodated. If a partner is unwilling and/or unable to accommodate something that you consider essential in a relationship, the relationship is unlikely to be successful as there will always be incompatibility. This latter point very much links to the sub-topics 'Unclarity about what we are looking for in a partner' and 'Accepting people as they are'.

2. Complacency is related to getting 'lazy' and not making any effort in a relationship once it is established. This can be related to an underlying belief that 'relationships should just work and not require any effort'. I have come to see that this isn't the case and that relationships require continuing effort from both parties. If one or both people in the relationship stops making effort, the relationship is likely to encounter problems and ultimately fail. Kelly Campbell, associate professor of psychology at California

State University in San Bernardino, explains, 'Complacency in relationships will lead to boredom and dissatisfaction, which are the key threats to infidelity and dissolution.' If we stop making an effort to spend quality time and do 'fun activities' with our partner, is it so surprising that the relationship may start to feel boring and unfulfilling?

3. I once went to a counsellor for a relationship problem, and after four sessions of listening to me, the counsellor asked, 'Kelvin, can you accept your partner as he is right now?' My answer was quite clearly, 'No.' The counsellor then firmly stated to me, 'Kelvin, he may always be that way.' On hearing that, I decided that she was correct as I had tried numerous times over many years to change him, and he was still the same, maybe worse now, and so I finished the relationship. I've come to see that a lot of people in relationships are doing what I was doing, hanging on, in the hope that their partner will one day be 'different'. As highlighted in the 'I'm sorry' hot topic, people can't be different until they understand the thinking and emotions driving their behaviour/actions. If someone is unwilling to look at the thoughts and emotions contributing to their behaviour, there is little chance of any change ever happening. In realising this, we can put our time and focus into finding a partner that is really compatible with us.

# Uncertainty

> 'Uncertainty is benign. Only a belief about uncertainty can cause emotions.'
> ~ K.Snaith

A common topic to enter the therapy room is that of 'uncertainty' and, in particular, how someone feels as a result of uncertainty.

Many of us can relate to feeling very 'uncertain' about some aspect or even many aspects of our life, which can cause us to feel quite 'unsettled'.

If this happens, it likely points to us holding a belief about uncertainty which can look a lot like this:

Uncertainty = Anxiety or 'not feeling good'

Or

I need to have certainty to feel okay.

Or

I can't feel okay with uncertainty.

I usually explain to my patients that uncertainty is actually 'benign', i.e., it doesn't have an energy to it. It is not even a thing that can be grasped. It's just an idea or understanding inside our head. Yet, from an early age, we may have learned from society, parents in particular, that uncertainty is a bad thing and something that we can't feel okay with.

The irony of believing the thought 'I need to have certainty to feel okay' is that you set yourself up to experience emotions and worry when it's not possible to gain certainty.

This then becomes a self-fulfilling prophecy.

Let's use a simple example to highlight this:

You take an interview for a job that you really want. The interviewer tells you at the end of the interview that she will ring you within the next 10 days to advise you of the result.

On leaving the interview room, 'uncertainty' starts to surface as you start to consider that you cannot know for sure if you have been successful in the interview until you receive the phone call. Furthermore, you cannot know when you will receive the phone call; it could be at any point in the next 10 days. Once uncertainty is detected by a mind that holds the belief 'I need to have certainty to feel okay', anxiety emotion is activated, and the mind may start to desperately think how it can gain certainty in order to feel better. It may start to run through all the possible ways of gaining certainty, maybe even replaying how you did in the interview, questions you got a bit stuck on and questions you answered well. This looks a lot like worrying. When all this is happening, you aren't dealing with the anxiety emotion in a healthy way, and so the emotion doesn't go away. This then serves to confirm the belief 'I need to have certainty to feel okay.' This belief is even further reinforced when you eventually receive the phone call from your interviewer and immediately start to feel relief.

How to break this cycle?

Whenever you start to detect uncertainty and/or the emotions associated with uncertainty, take a moment to apply your 'hands up and breathe' skill to the emotions in the body. Once the emotions have diffused, take a few minutes to continue breathing deeply whilst really connecting to the calm/peaceful feeling in the body. Whilst really keeping some awareness on this calm/peaceful feeling, gently invite your mind to notice that you are feeling 'okay' now and yet the 'uncertainty' in your life still remains. Let the mind observe how it is possible to be uncertain and 'feel okay'. Really take your time when doing this. This is the best way to restructure the erroneous belief that you 'can't feel okay with uncertainty'. You may need to repeat this process a couple more times whenever uncertainty surfaces to really help reinforce the new thinking.

This subject can also bring up a sub-topic of 'playing God/universe' in your life, which can cause the firing of emotions. If you notice that you may have started to play the role of God/universe in dictating how your life should look, ask yourself if you really want to take on this job. Also consider that things can take time to come into existence and that your journey of life may just not have allowed for what you want to happen yet. Equally, bad choices and actions may not have allowed for what you want to happen. Things are always the way they are supposed to be, until things are different, then they are the way they are supposed to be again.

When we really consider the subject of uncertainty, we see that our life is actually riddled with uncertainty all day long, every day and that it is really quite impossible to live a certain life. We can't even know if we will make it through the next hour or minute as our life could be ended by an unexpected asteroid falling from the sky or collapsing building!

When you have considered the sub-topic of 'Playing God/universe' in your life and applied the 'hands up and breathe' skill on your 'uncertainty' emotions, you start to see that uncertainty is really no problem at all and can even be quite exciting. As Eckhart Tolle points out, 'When you become comfortable with uncertainty, infinite possibilities open up in your life.'

# Addictions

*'Pick your weapon (emotional coping mechanism).'*
*~ K.Snaith*

Putting it simply, all addiction is caused by the erroneous conclusion that you need something in order to feel good.

When we haven't learned healthy emotional coping skills, we have to find another way of coping with our difficult emotions. The way we choose to cope (I call this 'weapon of choice') may be influenced by our immediate surroundings, interests, and belief about what is acceptable.

I will often do a simple exercise with my patients to help consider how we may have learned to cope with emotions when growing up. The exercise involves listing all of the key members of your family when growing up. Consider then what each member of your family did to cope with their emotions when you were growing up. An example of this from my own life may look like this:

Dad: Drinks alcohol (in pub and at home). Goes quiet and moody. Sleeps.

Mum: Worries. Goes to keep-fit classes and plays badminton.

Sister: Goes to the gym and works on her body. Eats a very strict and healthy diet to achieve her physique goals.

2nd Sister: Avoids talking about something. When angry with someone, cuts them off.

Brother: Sleeps. Eats sweets.

It's clear from this list what emotional coping mechanisms were presented to me in my immediate environment when growing up. Having seen how unhappy my dad seemed to be most of the time, I managed to conclude even as a child that his 'weapons of choice' (alcohol), going quiet and moody, and sleeping didn't seem to be working. My mum seemed to be a little bit more happy, although I was able to notice as a child how worrying seemed quite 'unhelpful'. My sister seemed to be doing the best and was the most happy person in my family when growing up with her 'gym and fitness obsession'. I can consider, in hindsight, that I therefore concluded that to be the best approach to managing emotions. With my sister's encouragement, I got into weight training and running from my early teenage years, which became my main emotional coping mechanism until I learned better ones in my late twenties. I also would utilise the worrying 'weapon' at times, which likely came from observing my mum. I recognised that it wasn't an effective strategy, but I didn't seem to have control over it at times.

It's easy for me to consider that if I didn't have my sister's influence when growing up, my emotional coping mechanisms might have looked very different. I would predict in hindsight that 'worrying' would have gotten out of control and that I would have ended up with quite a serious mental health problem at a young age if exercise had not come into the picture. Equally, I might have ended up resorting to alcohol as it was so socially acceptable and my father's 'weapon of choice'.

I'm also able to consider that if I had grown up in an environment with very different emotional coping mechanisms on display, for example, drugs, sex, smoking, or violence, I could have easily been influenced into utilising one of these.

How do we start to tackle addictions:

As already suggested, addictions are nothing more than 'unhealthy' emotional coping mechanisms, things we have learned to use to feel better. It's important to consider that all addictions work in providing short-term 'feeling good' or relief from emotions, but they are ineffective in offering long-term relief because they do not resolve the underlying thoughts and emotions.

The 'learned emotional coping' sheet in the Appendix section clearly highlights this.

To break an addiction, what we need to do is offer a 'better' emotional coping mechanism. The best emotional coping mechanism of all is the 'hands up and breathe' skill and 'questioning/answering your thoughts' skill. When this is learnt and starts to be applied when emotions are experienced, the need for addictions falls away. In this sense, we never need to try to get rid of an addiction but only work on improving our emotional coping through hands up and breathing and questioning/answering your thoughts skill.

From a thinking perspective, all addiction is likely to have similar thought structure, that is:

I need... (fill in with your weapon of choice)... in order to feel good.

We can practice reframing this belief to:

I don't need... (fill in with your weapon of choice) in order to feel good; What I need is to apply my hands up and breathing skill on the emotions I'm feeling in this moment. I can also apply my questioning/answering your thoughts skill if necessary.

I encourage all my patients to be 'gentle on themselves' when trying to break addictions. We are likely to 'default' to using strongly conditioned methods (weapons of choice) as these pathways are well trodden. I give the analogy of walking into our home through a grass garden that has two paths. One grass path is so well trodden down that it is very easy to go down that one (this represents our old weapon/s of choice). The new path (hands up and breathing and questioning/answering your thoughts) isn't so well trodden yet, and so it's still quite hard to make out the path. The more you apply hands up and breathing and questioning/answering your thoughts skill when you start to experience emotions, the more you tread on the grass, making the new pathway more clear. When you have trodden on the grass hundreds of times, the path becomes very clear and formed, and the old path can start to become overgrown and not so visible again.

# Obsessive-compulsive rituals/behaviour

'When you see that you can diffuse all of your emotions through hands up and breathing skill, the need to perform certain rituals or behaviours falls away.'
~ K.Snaith

Obsessive - compulsive rituals / behaviour commonly presents in the therapy room.

Some of these can be very strange and appear to have no logic at all. Like addictions, they are performed in order to make us feel good. They work as a 'distraction' from our emotions in the short term, which can help us to feel good but become ineffective in the long term because, like addictions, they are not addressing the underlying thoughts and emotions, and so the emotions return.

With obsessive-compulsive rituals/behaviour, it is important to first identify and write down all of your rituals/behaviour. Once you have a list, you will then need to prioritise which ritual/behaviour you would like to tackle first. I would suggest starting with just one ritual/behaviour and committing to working on that. Once you have successfully worked on that, you can move to the next, until you have worked on all of them.

How to do it:

Once you have decided on the first ritual/behaviour to tackle, identify when that ritual most commonly comes in. Write down when you expect it is likely to appear. This helps create more awareness of when you will need to do some work on it.

Quite simply, the treatment involves abstaining from doing the ritual that you want to do and instead applying the 'hands up and breathe' skill on the emotions and/or urges/sensations you feel inside the body.

The 'hands up and breathe' skill, when applied fully, has the power to show you that your emotions/urge/sensations will diffuse and that you can feel 'good' without having to do your ritual. Like the 'grass garden' analogy at the end of the 'Addictions' hot topic, the more times you use the 'hands up and breathe' skill to manage the emotions/urges/sensations, the clearer and more formed the pathway becomes and the other pathway (ritual/behaviour) starts to become overgrown and not so visible again. Like addictions, the ritual/behaviour falls away without you having to try to get rid of it when we focus on dealing with our emotions in a healthy way.

Obsessive-compulsive rituals/behaviour takes a lot of patience and persistence, particularly if someone has developed many. I always say, we can't tackle every ritual/behaviour at once. As the expression goes, 'Rome wasn't built in a day' and so let's start with 'one brick at a time'. Eventually, the building will be achieved. You have to be committed to tackling all of your rituals/behaviours because until they are all tackled, 'old thinking' remains and can continue to sprout and feed more rituals/behaviour.

I invite my patients to be 'gentle on themselves' the same as I do with addiction patients. It's important to consider that you are likely to 'default' to old pathways (rituals/behaviours) because they are well formed. However, when you notice you have defaulted to old pathways, just bring yourself back to applying your new methods. Remember, the more you tread on the grass, the clearer and more formed the pathway becomes. The less you tread on the grass, the less clear and formed the path will become.

The key thinking often involved with obsessive-compulsive rituals/behaviour:

I need to do… (fill in with your ritual/behaviour)… in order to feel good.

We can practice reframing this belief to:

I don't need to do (ritual/behaviour) in order to feel good; what I need to do is apply my hands up and breathing skill on the emotions and urges/sensations I'm feeling in this moment. I can also apply my questioning/answering your thoughts skill if needed.

I have found from experience when working with obsessive-compulsive rituals/behaviour that there is often an underlying 'big fear'. The fear can seem so big and scary that the person has never looked at it. The rituals serve as an attempt to get rid of the big emotions that have resulted from the 'fear'.

Applying the 'hands up and breathe' skill really is the best approach to managing the 'big fear'. The 'hands up and breathe' skill will show you that you can diffuse the emotions associated with the 'big' fear without having to do your ritual/behaviour. Furthermore, with more calm/peace, you will then be in a better position to consider the big fear. I've repeatedly found that the big fear isn't as scary after we have considered it more. In some cases, people can have a total change of thinking after doing hands up and breathing and carefully considering their fear. A good example of this would be a patient I once worked with who had many obsessive-compulsive 'rituals/behaviours' and a 'big' fear/worry that she may one day become a paedophile. The worry was so big for the girl that she totally avoided ever looking at the fear.

Instead, the girl would implement many rituals/behaviours under the guise that these were somehow 'protecting' her from becoming a paedophile. Once the girl had learned the 'hands up and breathe' skill and started to apply this on some of the big emotions connected to her fear, she was more able to discuss and consider the fear with me. One of the biggest concerns was if the girl became 'out of control' and started acting to harm children without her 'awareness' of it. The girl expressed, 'I wouldn't want to be arrested.' After expressing this belief, I asked the girl if this was really true that she wouldn't want to be arrested if she was 'out of control' and harming children. The girl realised that actually, she would want to be arrested if it meant this would stop more harm coming to children. All of a sudden, one of her worries had totally changed around. Another worry was how other people would respond if she was to become a paedophile, particularly her family. When considering this, we were able to consider that everyone has different beliefs about paedophiles and that some people may consider it 'an illness which someone has little choice over' and some people may consider paedophiles to just be 'evil people'. I asked the girl to consider what she thinks, and she said that she sways more towards them being 'evil people'. In expressing this, the girl was able to better understand why she would think other people may think this also and therefore worry about people's reaction if she was to become one. After further discussion about 'evil people' (please also see the specific hot topic on this), the girl was able to reconsider her view about paedophiles being 'evil people' and consider more that they may be 'very confused' and/or mentally ill people that have little 'choice' in their behaviour. All behaviour is driven by thinking. Confused thinking drives confused behaviour. This is a difficult subject for most people to consider. The girl managed to restructure several other thoughts when further considering her fear and started to feel much less worried and fearful about her 'big fear' happening. This really helped the girl in dropping most of her rituals/behaviours without having to even put much focus on them. Some, however, required more specific focus and tackling.

If obsessive-compulsive rituals/behaviour is a big problem for you, take your time to consider all of the pointers raised in this hot topic. Remember, 'Rome wasn't built in a day.' Likewise, it is going to take some time for you to be different. You will get there if you do the required work.

# Don't know what I want anymore

> 'What would you like to do if money was no object?'
> ~ Alan Watts

A very common theme to present in the therapy room is that of being a bit 'lost' and not having any vision for the future anymore. Sometimes life is tough, and money often plays a role in this. We can get so bogged down with just 'surviving' and trying to pay the bills each month that all of our hopes and dreams for the future can become buried.

I've worked with many patients who report having no vision for the future and don't really know what their hopes and dreams are anymore. The first thing I do with these patients is normalise this. I help my patients to understand that this is naturally going to happen when we have been in 'survival' mode for too long. I often will explain Maslow's hierarchy of needs model and how without the foundations of food, warmth, shelter, clothing, we cannot even start to think about creating our goals for the future.

If someone has been in 'survival' mode for too long, it's important for that person to reconnect with their goals and vision for the future.

A simple way I have found to help with this is to consider the millionaire question. This links to Alan Watt's question that is also highlighted in the hot topic on 'Career'.

The millionaire question looks like this:

You have paid for a few lines of numbers in the National Lottery because it is a rollover weekend for the third time and the jackpot is estimated to be around 100 million pounds.

You watch the tv eagerly as the winning numbers start to roll in, and to your utter disbelief, all of your numbers come up!

You have won the jackpot, and you are the only winner!

This is confirmed the next day, and the money is sent to your bank account. After a few days, 100 million pounds is now showing in your bank account balance. What are you going to do now?

Often when confronted with this question, my patients will laugh and poo poo the exercise as being stupid and pointless. If this happens, I usually explain to my patients again the reason we are doing this exercise, i.e., to reconnect to some hopes and dreams having been in survival mode for too long.

IMPORTANT NOTE:

It is important to pick the right time to do this exercise as if you are really stressed out and struggling to survive in your life, it may not be the right time to do this exercise. Your energy and focus may be much better spent on problem-solving how you are going to meet your bills for the month, etc. The time to do this exercise is when you are surviving quite well but are feeling quite 'lost' in knowing what you would like for the future.

When answering the question for the first time, people will often start by saying things like 'I'd buy a house, a nice car and take a nice holiday somewhere.' I will try to get people to give me as much detail as possible, and so I will often enquire, 'Where would you buy a house and what sort of a house would you buy? What car would you get? Where would you go on holiday?'

I will then explore with my patients what they would do after they have bought those nice things and taken a nice holiday.

It can be so difficult to do this exercise when we have been in survival mode for too long, and so I invite people to really take their time with answering this question. Furthermore, keep following forward with the imagining, past the 'material' purchases we may initially make. I often ask, 'When you have bought all those things and taken those holidays, how would you like to spend each day with 100 million pounds in your bank? What kind of food would you eat? Would you do any exercise, and if so, how often? Would you have a daily routine, and if so, what would it look like? Would you do any voluntary work or charity work? Would you continue to do paid work? Would you have any business ideas or plans you would do? Would you like to take up any new hobbies or old hobbies? Would you be dating or still be with your current partner?' The questions can go on and on...

Remember the whole purpose of this exercise is to let the mind start to dream again.

Let the mind start to fantasize again about what sort of a dream life it would like to have.

SECOND IMPORTANT NOTE:

This exercise should come with a warning, i.e., When you stop this exercise and come back to 'reality', it can be a little bit 'depressing'. Of course, this is understandable and a downside to doing the exercise, however, I would suggest that the benefits of reconnecting to your hopes and dreams for the future far outweigh a little bit of 'depressed' feeling.

The purpose of the exercise is to show us what kind of a life we would be having if money was no object. An interesting thing that I have found with every one of my patients that does this exercise is that there are many things in the 'dream vision' that do no require 100 million pounds in the bank. Often, the exercise can allow us to see that we may be able to achieve a very similar life for a fraction of the money, which can then be really encouraging for us to start working towards achieving this. Equally, we may see that we already have some of what we want in our dream life, which can be very satisfying.

I personally will do this exercise regularly, perhaps once a month, and sometimes even more regularly than that, as a way to check that my life is in alignment with my future hopes and dreams. I have found this to be very helpful in flagging up when changes may need to be made. As pointed out earlier, sometimes life can get busy and challenging, and we can get side-tracked with making choices that don't really fit with our hopes and dreams.

If you do find that you experience feelings of 'depression' after completing this exercise, you can apply your 'hands up and breathe' skill followed by the 'questioning/answering your thoughts' skill. This should help to diffuse the sadness and return you back to your peaceful self as you take the next steps towards achieving your future goals.

# Don't know why I'm feeling this way

> 'If there is a fire in your house, would you stand there whilst your house burns down and ponder what caused the fire?'
> ~ K.Snaith

If I received a pound every time I have heard the expression, 'I don't know why I'm feeling this way', I'd be a very rich man by now. This is such a common topic of discussion in my therapy room that I included it as a hot topic.

There is a perfect analogy I use when helping my patients to consider why they don't always understand what they are feeling. It is called the 'House on fire' analogy, and it goes like this:

HOUSE ON FIRE ANALOGY:

You return home from work one day, open your front door, and walk up the stairs to put some things away in your bedroom. On walking up the stairs, you discover that there is a huge fire spanning across all of the upstairs bedrooms and landing area.

I'm now going to give you three options, and I'd like for you to consider which one you would likely take

1. Reach for your phone and immediately call 999, asking for the fire brigade whilst you are leaving your property to ensure your safety.

2. Stand at the top of the stairs whilst all of the upstairs of your house is burning down and really ponder the question, 'What could have caused this fire?'

3. Leave the house and then distract yourself from the fire in your house by going to a nearby supermarket.

Hopefully, you are able to consider that taking the second or third option would be a little bit crazy. The obvious and sensible thing to do would be to call for the fire brigade whilst you wait outside to ensure your safety.

I usually ask my patients at this point: 'When there are 6ft high flames all around you, do you think you are going to be able to figure out what caused the fire?'

Equally, when the fire brigade arrives and you ask them what has caused the fire, do you think they are going to be able to answer you before they have put the fire out?

Hopefully, you are able to consider the impossibility of trying to figure out what caused the fire whilst there are 6-foot flames all around you. It's equally as impossible to try to figure out what caused the fire whilst you are in a nearby supermarket distracting yourself from the fire. Even the greatest firefighters of all time cannot ascertain exactly what has caused a fire until they have put the fire out.

I then point out to my patients that in this analogy, our body is like the house and the emotions are like the flames. How many of us when our house is on fire, i.e., emotions are burning fiercely in the body, sit or stand there desperately trying to figure out what caused the fire (emotions)? Are you able to consider the impossibility of what you would be asking and, therefore, how confusing this would be? Equally, how many of us when we are experiencing strong emotions distract ourselves by doing something else, yet then worry and get very distressed because we are unable to understand why we are feeling the way we are feeling?

I, therefore, advise when the flames are high to just focus on putting out the fire! All else is crazy!

The best strategy always to put out the fire is the 'hands up and breathe' skill. This is equivalent to spraying water from huge hose pipes onto the fires. Continue with hands up and breathing until the flames have been put out.

Once the fires have been put out, the fire brigade can easily survey the scene to try to ascertain the cause of the fire. Likewise, once our flames (emotions) have been put out, we are more able to consider what just happened, i.e., what thinking was playing to trigger such strong emotions.

I usually then ask my patients, 'Do you think it would be helpful for the fire brigade to tell us what the cause of the fire was? If so, why?'

The usual answer I get is, 'Yes, of course, so that we can then stop the fire from happening again.'

I then highlight that humans are the same, i.e., if we can figure out the cause (the thinking) and reappraise our thoughts by using the 'questioning/answering your thoughts' skill, then we can potentially stop the fire (emotions) from coming back again.

# Feeling numb

> 'If you are feeling numb, you have simply stopped feeling in an attempt to deal with your emotions.'
> ~ K.Snaith

Quite a common problem to present in the therapy room is that of feeling 'numb'. I have found from experience that this happens when someone's emotions become so overwhelming that they almost 'dissociate' from their body in an attempt to cope. Another way of saying this would be that someone just 'blocks off' or totally ignores their feelings in an attempt to feel better.

I always advise my patients who are experiencing this that it is actually quite an intelligent thing to do if you don't have any other emotional coping mechanisms because it does help you to calm down. The only problem with this method (which is often unconscious and not something we choose to do) is that it comes with a big price, i.e., we don't get to feel any 'good' feelings either.

I often state the quote to my patients: 'It's like throwing out the baby with the dirty bathwater.' The dirty bathwater in this quote would represent the strong emotions we are feeling, and the baby would represent the good feeling of our essence. When we stop feeling in the body in an attempt to cope with the difficult emotions, we also then lose the capacity to feel any good feeling.

What to do?

If this is happening for you, the first thing to recognise is that it is quite simply your mind's attempt to try and cope with the difficult emotions you are experiencing. It is not wrong that you are doing this, but it isn't the most effective method to cope with difficult feelings. Learning the 'hands up and breathe' and 'questioning/answering your thoughts' skills gives you a much better option when difficult emotions arise.

Before we can start applying the 'hands up and breathe' skill to the difficult emotions we are experiencing, we first need to re-connect to them! To do this, I usually advise using the simple 'body scan' exercise.

BODY SCAN EXERCISE:

Consider that you are inside a microscopic submarine which is going to sail the length of your body, starting from your toes and going all the way through the body until it reaches the top of the head. Remember that submarines are designed to sail whilst completely submerged in deep water, and so you will need to imagine that you are deep inside your body, not just at the surface.

Some questions I ask when doing this: What temperature is the water (blood) that you are submerged in? Is the water choppy or quite still? What colour is the water? Can you give any words to the feeling of the water?

Hopefully, this simple analogy gets you feeling deep into your body again. What may happen very quickly when starting this is that you start to reconnect again to some difficult feelings/emotions. This is when you will need to apply your 'hands up and breathe' skill. Remember, always deal with the fire first before looking into the cause of the fire. Just spend some time feeling and scanning up your body from your toes to the top of your head whilst you continue to do the 'hands up and breathe' skill to anything you notice whilst scanning.

IMPORTANT NOTE: The submarine analogy is to help you consider what you are trying to do with this exercise. It is important that you don't just use 'imagination' when doing this exercise as the whole purpose of it is to reconnect to the 'feeling' inside the body.

If you find that you are struggling to feel anything when starting this exercise, I would recommend that you spend a good five minutes just focussing on one area of your body to begin with. This could be, for example, your left foot or knee. Really get used to connecting to the 'feeling' in that area of your body before moving into other areas of the body. When you have covered the whole of the body from toes to head, you have completed the 'body scan' exercise.

# Panic

> 'The problem with panic is that we don't want it, possibly more than any other feeling or emotion. Until we can look forward to experiencing panic, our work is not done.'
> ~ K.Snaith

Panic or panic attacks often present as a problem in my therapy room. A panic attack is extreme anxiety, which can result in shortness of breath/struggling to breathe, tension, a tight chest, a pounding heart, racing mind, and feeling really hot/sweaty.

When panic presents in my therapy room, there's one piece of advice I always give: To resist panic is to resist reality (what is happening) and to resist reality is hopeless, we will always lose.

HANDS UP TO THE PANIC:

If someone is experiencing panic attacks, I always advise that they need to start applying the 'hands up and breathe' skill as soon as the panic starts to arise. Furthermore, applying the 'hands up and breathe' and 'questioning/answering your thoughts' skills on other emotions that arise throughout the day will ensure we have more peace/calm, which is likely to prevent panic from happening in the first place.

Putting your hands up to panic means putting your hands up to all of the physical sensations, symptoms, and emotion/s or energy that you feel in the body during panic. This can seem a very scary thing to do at first. I can assure you that no harm will ever come from allowing the panic symptoms to be as they are. Resisting panic symptoms is likely to make them worse and keep them coming back again and again. I encourage patients to try to take a 'curious' approach to their panic symptoms, simply watching how 'high' or 'strong' they can get rather than trying to stop them from getting stronger or higher or remove them altogether.

TOY CAR ANALOGY:

I encourage my patients to consider that their physical symptoms/sensations are likened to a child's toy car. Imagine you put the toy car down on a very big kitchen floor. You give the car a really hard push whilst simultaneously letting go of the car to allow it to roll across the kitchen floor. The car zooms across the kitchen floor and reaches its maximum speed. What will happen to the car after it reaches its maximum speed? Hopefully, you were able to consider that it would start to slow down because there is no force pushing it anymore. Similarly, when we hands up to our panic symptoms, they reach their maximum 'speed' and then start to slow down because there is no force 'driving' them anymore.

The more we apply hands up and breathing on our panic symptoms, the more we learn that all physical sensations/symptoms after reaching their maximum 'speed' will start to fall. We discover that it is never dangerous to allow symptoms to 'max out' and actually is the quickest way for them to pass. Feeling some calm/peace having applied hands up and breathing to panic symptoms gives us the best evidence that 'everything is okay'.

Trying to give specific pointers about the thinking that may be driving someone's panic is difficult as everyone is so different. I have found from experience that the hot topics on 'Health anxiety and death' and 'Worst shame and forgiving self' may be particularly relevant for people experiencing panic. Panic appears to be linked to the subject of 'death' because when we experience the physical symptoms of restricted breathing and a pounding heart, we can easily start to believe we are going to die of a heart attack or suffocation. If we have not examined our thoughts about death and are not 'okay' with dying, then high anxiety and panic can arise. If we were 'okay' with dying, then we may not react with the same heightened anxiety and panic to the thought that we could die. Social reputation may be another key factor in panic. If we start to believe that our social reputation is going to be ruined, and we don't want this to happen, it's easy to understand how anxiety and panic would arise. If we were 'okay' with our social reputation being ruined, perhaps we wouldn't react in the same way to a thought about this happening.

# Conclusion and well wishes

### Till death do us part. . .

Thank you for taking the time to read this book and give yourself the best chance of attaining good mental health for life.

I'm confident that if you have read this book carefully, you now have everything you need to achieve great mental health.

To achieve anything in life, some effort and focus is required. The more focus and effort you give to applying your newly learned knowledge and skills, the better results you will achieve.

Eventually, you come to see that peace, love, happiness, joy, and feeling good is what you are, and there is absolutely nothing you can do to change this. What you seek is already yours. The diamond necklace that you have been searching the house for was around your neck the whole time!

When you realise this simple truth, life becomes really simple. You live your life with peace as you take each step towards your next goal. You never need to be anything other than what you are. Every emotion becomes a great blessing and guide from beyond.

The hot topics covered in this book are not meant to be an exhaustive list of topics that can occur in mental health problems. Equally, the pointers given for each topic are not meant to be exhaustive. The topics chosen are simply my most commonly experienced topics over the last five years of therapy, and the pointers chosen are my main learning points. I never ask you to believe me but to hold what I have written with a light grasp whilst you test out and discover for yourself.

If this book proves helpful for you, I hope that you will discuss it with your friends, family, loved ones, and even enemies. Your enemies may need it more than your loved ones.

More peace in the world starts with you. Be the change that you want to see in the world, and the rest of the world will follow. Together, we can achieve a more peaceful planet.

I'm sending you so much love right now (without choice).

Kelvin xox

# Appendices

- Learned emotional coping handout
- Questioning your statements handout
- Model for all non-organic psychological illness handout
- Soup of the mind handout
- Joining the dots handout

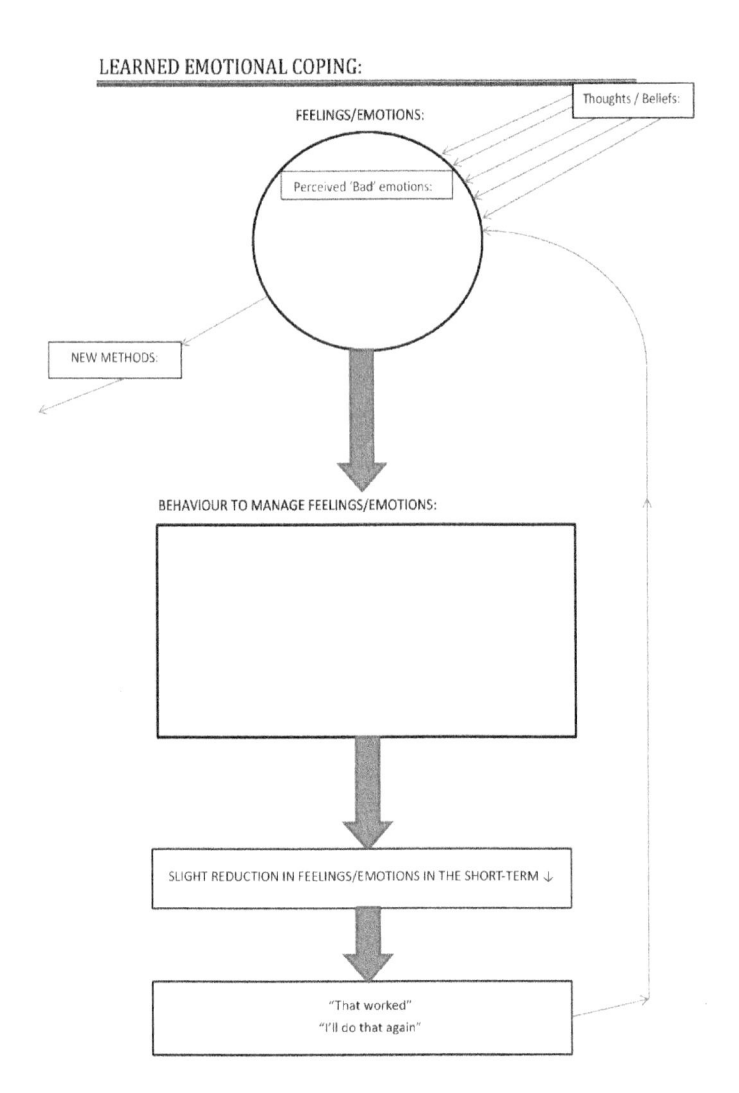

## LEARNED EMOTIONAL COPING:

**FEELINGS/EMOTIONS:**

Thoughts / Beliefs:

Perceived 'Bad' emotions:

NEW METHODS:

**BEHAVIOUR TO MANAGE FEELINGS/EMOTIONS:**

SLIGHT REDUCTION IN FEELINGS/EMOTIONS IN THE SHORT-TERM ↓

"That worked"
"I'll do that again"

# Questioning Your Statements

The following questions can help you consider how a statement is affecting you and open up the mind to other more helpful thoughts (appraisals) about a particular subject. First identify and write down the statement that you would like to explore. Consider: Where do you see yourself, others or the world as less than perfect? Where has life got it wrong? What advice would you offer? These questions may help you to identify some statements that you hold and could explore. Are 'what if' type worries arising? If they are then you will need to answer the 'what if' worry in order to reveal the deeper/actual worry.

Pick up your scrap paper, diary or notebook and write the statements down at the top of the page. Then work through the following questions answering honestly and taking plenty of time to consider each question.

1. Is it true? (Answering this question can show you if you believe this thought or not)

2. Can you absolutely know for sure that it's true? (Answering this question can help you to consider how

much you believe this thought. You may like to consider here if can we know anything for sure.)

3. How does it make you feel when you believe this thought is true? (Answering this question can help you to connect the emotions/feelings/physical sensations that come with this belief).

4. How does it make you behave when you believe this thought is true? (Answering this question can help you to connect the behaviours that come with this thought).

5. Who would you be / how would you feel without this thought? (Answering this question can allow you to consider what you would be like and what your life might look like if you didn't have this thought: imagine that you or someone else is capturing that thought between their hands so that you no longer have it in your head)

6. Is there any benefit to believing this thought, given how it seems to make you feel/behave? (Answering this question allows you to really consider the benefit that this thought is bringing you . How is it serving you?)

7. Do you have or can you see any concerns about not having this thought any more? (Answering this question can help you consider why the mind is continuing to believe this thought)

8. What is the direct opposite to this thought? (Answering this question can help the mind open up to a total opposite position which may never have been considered/given any airtime. Could this thought be just as true? Can you dig deep (take your time) and find any examples to support this opposite thought?)

9. What is the the middle ground or more balanced thought here? (Use the original and opposite thought to consider a thought which might include/encompass both. How does this sit (feel) with you? Given what you have considered, which thought seems to be the most accurate/truthful now?)

**This is the revised version of Byron Katie's 4 questions. Please visit www.thework.com for more information.**

MODEL FOR ALL NON-ORGANIC PSYCHOLOGICAL ILLNESS.
K. Snaith

**EXPERIENCE:**

PAIN (PHYSICAL)
EMOTIONS
THOUGHTS
IMAGES/MENTAL VIDEOS
SOUNDS / VOICES

**REJECTION OF EXPERIENCE:**

"I don't want this"

**GOOD MENTAL HEALTH FOR LIFE**

HANDS UP THERAPY SKILL, QUESTIONING AND ANSWERING YOUR THOUGHTS SKILL AND PROBLEM SOLVING / TAKING ACTION

POINT OF INTERVENTION

**ATTEMPT TO AVOID EXPERIENCE:**

DRUGS/ALCOHOL
DISTRACTION
PHARMACEUTICAL
AVOIDANCE OF THINGS
SLEEPING
WORRYING/RUMINATING

**TEMPORARY RELIEF FROM EXPERIENCE:**

**NO LEARNING: BELIEFS REMAIN INTACT & NO PROBLEM SOLVING**

RE-TRIGGERING

## Soup of the Mind

If you find yourself feeling 'overwhelmed' or 'stressed-out' then it is time for you to pick up your pen and paper and break down what's going on in your life and mind into smaller subject areas. This is a bit like figuring out all of the ingredients that go into the 'soup'. This simple exercise can really help you to feel clearer about what's going on in your life and mind and will enable you to then start working on each subject area (one at a time).

LIST BELOW ALL OF THE MAIN SUBJECT AREAS IN YOUR LIFE THAT ARE LIKELY RUNNING THROUGH YOUR MIND RIGHT NOW. THIS ONLY REQUIRES YOU IDENTIFYING THE BIG SUBJECT AREAS IN YOUR LIFE AND NOT GOING INTO ANY DETAIL ABOUT EACH SUBJECT YET:

_____

_____

_____

_____

_____

Now take your time to complete a 'Joining the dots' sheet for each of the subject areas you have listed.

# Joining the Dots

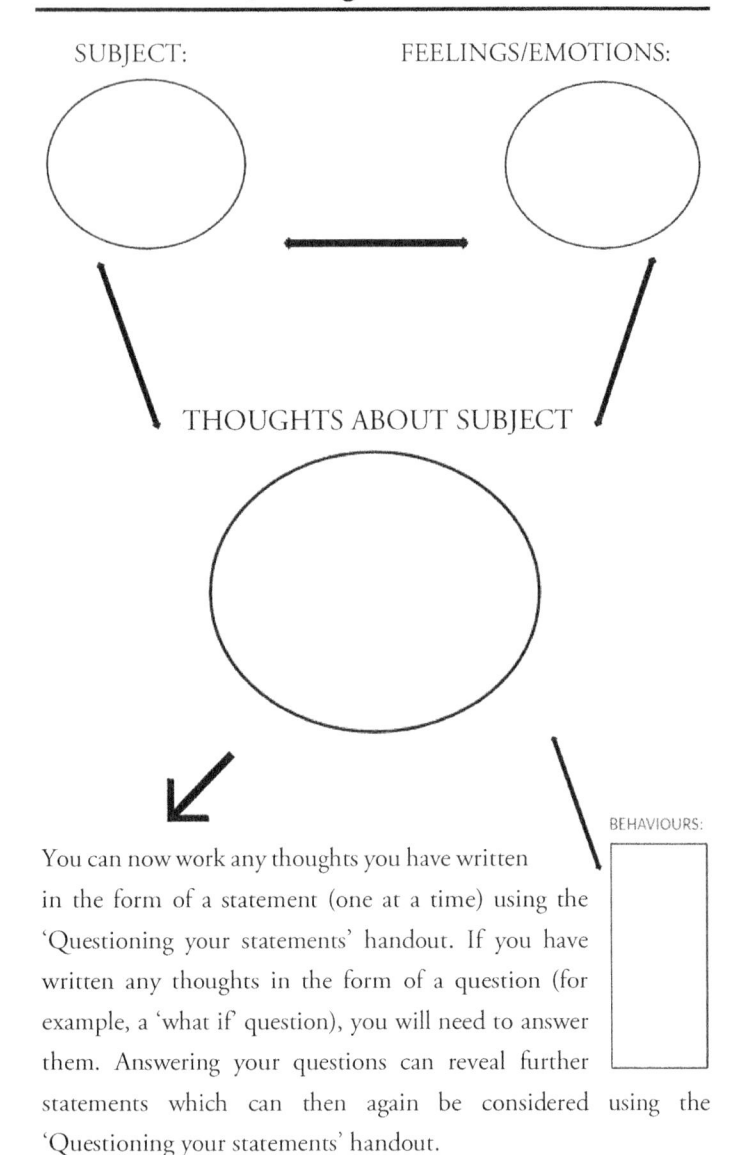

SUBJECT:   FEELINGS/EMOTIONS:

THOUGHTS ABOUT SUBJECT

BEHAVIOURS:

You can now work any thoughts you have written in the form of a statement (one at a time) using the 'Questioning your statements' handout. If you have written any thoughts in the form of a question (for example, a 'what if' question), you will need to answer them. Answering your questions can reveal further statements which can then again be considered using the 'Questioning your statements' handout.

Printed in Great Britain
by Amazon